Photoshop Web Magic, Volume 1

Photoshop Web Magic, Volume 1

TED SCHULMAN, RENÉE LEWINTER,
AND TOM EMMANUELIDES

Hayden
Books

Photoshop Web Magic, Volume 1

Library of Congress Catalog Number: 96-77851
ISBN: 1-56830-314-9

Printed in the United States of America   3 4 5 6 7 8 9 0

Warning and Disclaimer

This book is sold as is, without warranty of any kind, either express or implied. While every precaution has been taken in the preparation of this book, the authors and Hayden Books assume no responsibility for errors or omissions. Neither is any liability assumed for damages resulting from the use of the information or instructions contained herein. It is further stated that the publisher and authors are not responsible for any damage or loss to your data or your equipment that results directly or indirectly from your use of this book.

The Photoshop Web Magic Team

Publisher
Jordan Gold

Executive Editor
Beth Millett

Copy/Production Editor
Kevin Laseau

Technical Editor
Susan Aronoff

Cover Designer
Karen Ruggles

Book Designers
Renée LeWinter
Gary Adair

Production Team Supervisors
Laurie Casey, Joe Millay, Gina Rexrode

Production Team
Trina Brown, Daniel Caparo, Maureen Hanrahan,
Aleata Howard, Linda Knose, Christopher Morris,
Scott Tullis, Megan Wade, Pamela Woolf

Composed in *Goudy* and *Syntax*
Some thumbtab imagery provided by CMCD, Digital Stock,
D'Pix, FotoSets, Image Club Graphics, and PhotoDisc, 1995.

About the Authors

Ted Schulman has 20 plus years of experience as an award-winning producer, director, and developer of over 250 multimedia, video, and film projects. His clients have included leading Fortune 500 companies.

Since 1992, Ted has combined his background in social anthropology with Internet development. He focuses on the creation of community-based Web sites to help bring advanced communications to underserved communities.

Ted can be found on the Web at TSPI.com (email address ts@tspi).

Renée LeWinter is an artist, print, and multimedia designer and computer imaging consultant. For more than 20 years she has worked with software developers to foster the evolution of the digital studio.

Renée's articles have appeared in leading trade publications where she writes about the creative style, business, and technology trends that impact artists and designers.

Renée is represented on the World Wide Web by the 911 Gallery http://www.911Gallery.org/911/.

Tom Emmanuelides founded THAT Agency, an interactive new media company, where for the last 7 years he has served as president and creative director.

Based in New York City, Tom has applied his multidisciplinary skills to interface design, programming interactive titles, and advanced multimedia Web development. Tom also does consulting for local and international companies addressing the Internet market.

Tom can be reached at THATAGENCY.com.

Trademark Acknowledgments

Dedication

For Meril, Julia, and Peter for their support and patience—Ted

For my mother—Renée

My Mother and Father, in memory of Richard L. Heinrich, Viola S. Goodsir and Mark M. Monolides—Tom

Acknowledgments

Special Contributors

Carrie Notte

Robert Desbiens

Special Thanks to:

Cynthia Baron, Robert DeBenedictis, Betty Gerisch, Laurence LeWinter, Douglas Mitchell, Michael Nolan, Chris Schiavo, Marian Schiavo and Greg Simsic

We would like to thank our team at Hayden Books—Melanie Rigney, Beth Millett, Kevin Laseau, Susan Aronoff, and the Macmillan design group.

Hayden Books

The staff of Hayden Books is committed to bringing you the best computer books. What our readers think of Hayden is important to our ability to serve our customers. If you have any comments, no matter how great or how small, we'd appreciate your taking the time to send us a note.

You can reach Hayden Books at the following:

Macmillan Computer Publishing
Web Design and Graphics
201 West 103rd Street
Indianapolis, IN 46290
317-581-3833

Visit our Web site at http://www.mcp.com

Contents at a Glance

Contents

Introduction

Photoshop has become an indispensable tool for Web page design. Search through the Web and in site after site, there are examples of dynamic Web graphics created with Photoshop.

Photoshop Web Magic, Volume 1 presents easy to use recipes for creating those Web page graphics. Use the colorful thumbtabs to browse through the book to find techniques, hints, and tips for designing custom backgrounds, buttons, titles, menus bars, rules, icons, and animations that can enhance and improve your Web site.

Whether you are a designer or a programmer, interested in creating Web pages for your business or for personal expression, *Photoshop Web Magic, Volume 1* shows you how to add a professional flair to your Web site. Don't forget to check out Appendix A, where we have included some of our favorite bookmarks locating design resources and downloadable shareware graphics collections.

Hope to see you on the Web!

Ted Schulman

Renée LeWinter

Tom Emmanuelides

Before You Start

Welcome

This book was not meant to be an introductory guide to Photoshop or the World Wide Web. Even if you are new to Photoshop or the Web, you will still be able to find lots of useful information. Regardless of your level of experience, this book will help you to build dynamic Web graphics with easy-to-follow instructions. If you possess a general understanding of Photoshop but may need the occasional reminder, Photoshop Basics will help refresh your memory on fundamental tasks without slowing you down.

System Setup

Adobe recommends 32MB of RAM for Power Macintosh and Windows 3.1, Windows 95, or Windows NT. If you are running a 68030-based Macintosh, Adobe recommends 24MB of RAM, but we suggest that you add extra memory if you can afford it. The new Photoshop 4.0 filters and other third-party software will push your system to its limits. If you plan to do Web design and development professionally, then consider this yardstick. You will be using your system software + Photoshop + HTML editor + word processor + Web navigator + fonts + email +... all open at the same time. Add all these together and you will have a barometer of your memory needs.

Photoshop 4.0 is shipping exclusively on CD-ROM, so it is important that you have a CD-ROM drive. Have lots of storage and consider purchasing at least a two gigabyte hard drive and an alternative external removable drive for back-up. You will be building a large library of pictures and graphics.

We also recommend using Photoshop 4.0 or later because we used many of the new 4.0 features such as the Actions palette to write this book. If you are still working with 3.05 or an earlier version, check out the Photoshop Basics section before using this book. Adobe made changes in the Photoshop 4.0 interface including the toolbar and we followed the new interface in our instructions. Keep in mind that if you are duplicating our examples with an earlier version of Photoshop, your results may not exactly match ours.

Adobe Photoshop 4.0

Adobe Photoshop 4.0 for Apple Macintosh and Microsoft Windows platforms introduced several key new features. These include the Actions palette; Adjustment Layers; Free Transform; a new Navigator palette; Guides and Grids; 48 artistic filters, and custom, multicolor Gradients. Also of particular interest to Web designers are the following new features.

Copyright Protection Adobe introduces digital watermarking, using Imagemarc software developed by Digimarc Corporation. This feature enables creative professionals who plan to post their images on the Web, to protect the copyright by embedding an imperceptible, digital watermark in each image. This watermark, not apparent to the human eye, is still readable even after an image has been edited, or printed and rescanned. Adobe Photoshop will recognize the watermarked file when it is opened and will verify that the image is held under copyright.

New Web File Formats Adobe Photoshop 4.0 introduces support for three new Web file formats.

> ➡   Portable Network Graphics (PNG)—A new RGB file format

> ➡   Progressive JPEG—Including new user controls over JPEG settings

> ➡   Portable Document Format (PDF)—The Adobe Acrobat format

These new formats are in addition to version 3.0 support for transparent, interlaced GIF files with the GIF 89a plug-in. These new formats are explained in detail in the Adobe manual and at the Adobe Web site.

Web Access to Adobe Remember to check out Adobe's Web site on the World Wide Web. Their address is `http://www.adobe.com`. The site is updated frequently, and we find it useful for locating information about Adobe products, user groups, and software demos and updates. Abode also provides a calendar of special events and conferences that they sponsor.

Conventions

Resolution and Color

To create graphics in Photoshop for the Web you will want to work in RGB mode and set the file resolution to 72 dpi. Unless otherwise noted all files were created with white backgrounds as a default setting. Because we had to prepare our examples for printing on paper, we set our file resolution to 150 dpi for the variations and 300 dpi for the thumbtabs. Our colors may not match exactly what you are seeing on-screen since we converted our RGB files to CMYK. Our colors are noted in the book in RGB (0, 0, 0).

File Size and Download Times

The smaller the file size the faster the download time. Remember that one Web page may contain several graphic elements and each must download before your Web page is completed. Also, do not assume that Web surfers have fast modems. The average Web surfer is still using a 14.4 modem and not the faster 28.8. If you can manage, make your files 30K or smaller and take advantage of Netscape's and Microsoft's support of layering in their browsers. Layering enables you to build more complex graphics by overlapping several graphic files on top of each other when you download a page. This way you can avoid blank screens.

The Adobe Photoshop 4.0 manual has a detailed chapter on Saving and Exporting Images. Check out our bookmarks list in Appendix A for online resources for finding the most up-to-date information. The Web is a perpetually moving target where technical specifications are concerned. Microsoft, Netscape, and other browser developers are continuing to update and change their software. Look for more Java applets and third-party plug-ins for animation, video, and sound.

The Toolbox

Occasionally in this book we have used a third-party filter or a specially prepared preset file. Any of these extra tools that are not included standard with Photoshop 4.0 are listed in the Toolbox in the lower-left corner of the first page of each technique. The Toolbox lists everything you'll need to create each effect and any of its variations. The CD-ROM that comes with this book contains all of the files needed to perform all of the basic techniques. For information on accessing these files, turn to Appendix C, "What's on the CD-ROM."

The Steps

The Blue Type As you work through the steps you will see phrases that are colored a light blue. The same phrases are listed in alphabetical order in the Photoshop Basics section. If the phrase in blue asks you to perform a task that you are unfamiliar with, then you can find that phrase in the Photoshop Basics section, followed by instructions on how to perform that task. Advanced users may simply perform the task as normal.

Menu Commands You will also see instructions that look like this:

Filter➡Blur➡Gaussian Blur (2 pixels)

This example asks you to apply the Gaussian Blur filter. To perform this command, click the Filter menu at the top of the screen and drag down to Blur. When Blur is highlighted, a new menu will open to the right from which you can choose Gaussian Blur.

3

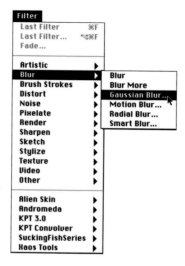

In this example, a dialog box appears that asks you for more information. All of the settings needed to perform each task appear in the text of the instruction step. The example above is telling you to enter 2 pixels as the Radius.

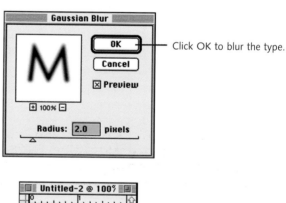

Click OK to blur the type.

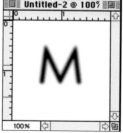

Settings Following each action in the steps are settings for you to use with that feature. These settings are meant to act as guides; the best settings for your Web graphic may vary. For starters, begin with the settings that you see in the figures as you proceed through the technique. Although we tried to use settings that would work for 72 dpi screen resolution, we were constrained by the needs of print reproduction. As a rule of thumb, if it looks good on your monitor it will probably work. If you do need to adjust your monitor, set your settings lower. The following two images demonstrate the importance of adjusting for resolution differences. A 5-pixel Radius Gaussian Blur was applied to both images.

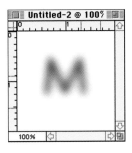

150 DPI

300 DPI

Tips   Occasionally in this book you'll also see some paragraphs of text that have been separated out to create Tips. Tips are additional bits of information that can help you render a better effect by providing more information beyond the basic steps of each lesson.

Photoshop Basics

How to Use This Section

This part of the book is intended to help new and novice users of Photoshop with the simple, basic tasks required to do the Web graphics we have created. Each of these tasks corresponds to the text highlighted in blue, so users can easily find the instructions they need in this chapter.

This chapter proceeds on two assumptions: that you're creating our Web graphics in Photoshop 4.0, and that you're keeping the Tool and Layer/Channel/Path palettes open. If one or both of the Tool and Layer/Channel/Path palettes are closed when you refer to this chapter, you can reopen them by name using the Window menu at the top of the screen. If you're using an earlier version of Photoshop, you can refer to the Photoshop manual for instructions on how to perform these tasks—also keep in mind that Photoshop 2.5 does not offer the ability to work in layers.

Please note that keyboard shortcuts for Adobe Photoshop for Windows appear between brackets [].

The Tools Palette

If you're not familiar with Photoshop's Tool palette, there's no reason to panic. With a bit of experimentation, it doesn't take long to learn each tool's individual functions. To help the beginning Photoshop user along the way, here is a representation of the toolbars from both Photoshop 3.0 and 4.0. This will also help advanced users find the rearranged tools.

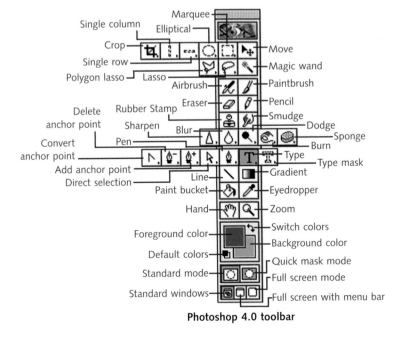

Photoshop 4.0 toolbar

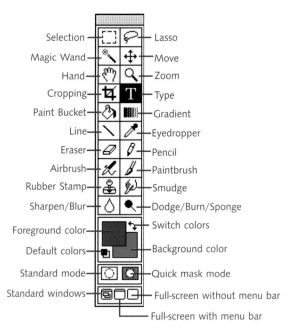

Photoshop 3.0 toolbar

Basic Photoshop Tasks

Add a Vertical/Horizontal Guide

Shortcut: Press Command-; [Control-;] to Show Guides and press Command-R [Control-R] to Show Rulers.

To add a vertical or horizontal guide, choose View➡Show Guides and View➡Show Rulers.

With any tool selected, drag a guide from either the horizontal or vertical ruler. To align the guide with a ruler position, hold down the Shift key as you drag the guide.

TIP As you drag the guide, hold down the Option [Alt] key to switch between horizontal or vertical guides, or vice versa.

Choose a Foreground or Background Color

Shortcuts: Press D to change the colors to their defaults (black for the foreground, white for the background).

Press X to switch the foreground and background colors.

To change the foreground or background color click the Foreground or Background icon.

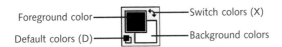

Foreground color — Switch colors (X)
Default colors (D) — Background colors

The Color Picker dialog box appears, enabling you to choose a new foreground or background color by moving and clicking the cursor (now a circle) along the spectrum box, or by changing specific RGB, CMYK, or other percentage values. Note that the Foreground and Background icons on the Tool palette now reflect your color choices.

9

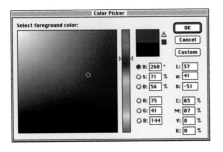

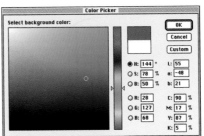

Convert to a New Mode

To convert from one color mode to another color mode, click on the Image menu at the top of the screen and scroll down to the Mode selection, then scroll down to select your mode of preference. For example, if you wanted to switch from CMYK mode to RGB mode, you would choose Image➡Mode➡RGB. The check mark to the left of CMYK will move up to RGB, indicating you are now in RGB mode.

TIP Remember, there is a different range of colors available for each color mode. For example, no matter what color mode the file is in on screen, your printer (if it prints in color) is going to print your work in CMYK. Since the color ranges for RGB and CMYK are different, you should convert your RGB image to CMYK before printing. Otherwise, you may be in for a big surprise when your bright green prints as a dull tan.

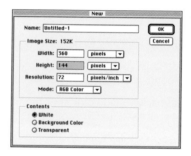

Create/Edit a Grid

To create or edit a grid, choose File➡Preferences➡Guides and Grids, and use the dialog box to set your preferences.

Create a Layer Mask

To create a layer mask, choose Layer➔Add Layer Mask, and choose either Reveal All (white) or Hide All (black). For the purposes of the effects in this book, always choose Reveal All. A layer mask is used to mask out, or hide, specified parts of a layer.

Create an Adjustment Layer

Shortcuts: Command-click [Control-click] the new layer icon on the Layers palette.

This is a new feature available only in Photoshop 4.0. To create an adjustment layer, choose Layer➔New➔Adjustment Layer. If you want to confine the effects of the color and tonal adjustments to a selected area, make a selection before creating the layer.

11

Use the New Adjustment Layer dialog box to establish your adjustment options and settings.

Create a New Channel

Shortcuts: Click the new channel icon on the Channels palette.

To create a new channel, choose New Channel from the Channels palette pop-up menu.

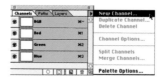

Use the Channel Options dialog box to establish your settings. Unless otherwise noted, we have always used Photoshop's defaults when creating a new channel. This figure shows Photoshop's default settings.

Create a New File

Shortcuts: Press Command-N [Control-N].

To create a new file, choose File➔New. The New dialog box appears, where you can name your new file and establish other settings. See "Before You Start," for information on the conventions we used when creating new files for the Web graphic examples in this book.

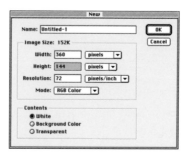

Create a New Layer

Shortcuts: Click the New Layer icon on the Layers palette.

To create a new layer, choose New Layer from the Layer palette pop-up menu, or choose Layer➔New➔Layer.

The New Layer dialog box opens, enabling you to name the new layer and establish other settings.

Delete a Channel

To delete a channel, go to the Channels palette, select the channel you want to delete, and drag it to the Trash icon at the lower-right corner—just like you would get rid of a document on the desktop by dragging it to the Trash. You can also select the channel you want to delete and choose Delete channel from the Channels palette pop-up menu.

 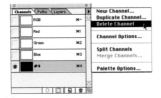

13

Deselect a Selection

Shortcut: Press Command-D [Control-D].

To deselect a selection, choose Select➔None. The marquee disappears. Switching selection tools will also deselect a selection.

Duplicate a Channel

Shortcut: Click the channel you want to duplicate, and drag it on top of the new channel icon.

To create a duplicate of a channel, make the channel active, then select Duplicate Channel from the Channels palette pop-up menu.

This creates a new copy of the channel you selected for duplication and causes the Duplicate Channel dialog box to appear.

Enter/Exit Quick Mask

Shortcuts: Press Q to enter and exit Quick Mask mode.

Click the Quick Mask icon to switch to Quick Mask mode and the Standard mode icon to return to Standard mode.

Essentially a Quick Mask is a temporary channel. When you're in Quick Mask mode you can use any of Photoshop's tools and functions to change the selection without changing the image. When you switch back to Standard mode you'll have a new selection.

Enter the Text

There are two type tools in Photoshop 4.0—the standard Type tool and the Type Mask tool. Each effect in this book specifies which type tool to use.

14

Before entering the text using the standard Type tool, make sure the foreground color is set to the color you want the text to be. If you are entering text into a layer, then the standard Type tool creates a new layer for the type.

The Type Mask tool creates selection outlines of the text you enter without filling them with a new color and without creating a new layer.

To enter the text, select the type tool you want to use, and then click anywhere in the image to open the Type Tool dialog box. Type the text in the large box at the bottom of the dialog box, and make your attribute choices from the options above. Unless noted otherwise in the instructions, always make sure you have the Anti-Aliased box checked.

After clicking OK, move the type into position with the Marquee (Type Mask tool) tool.

Export to GIF Format

To export to a GIF format, choose File➡Export➡GIF89a Export. Use the GIF89a format for graphics with transparent areas. In the dialog box choose either the Exact, Adaptive or System Palette (GIF supports a maximum of 256 colors). If you created a custom palette, click Load to locate and select your custom palette. Consult your Photoshop manual or *Designing Web Graphics* by Lynda Weinman for a more detailed discussion of color palette options versus file sizes.

15

The adaptive palette displays the best results for continuous tone images. Here are two examples (shown in the GIF89a preview window) where the adaptive palette was limited to 128 colors and 16 colors.

TIP A new alternative to the GIF format is the PNG format. Unlike GIF, PNG keeps all color information in an image, uses a lossless compression scheme, supports alpha channels, and enables you to specify how transparent areas will look. Choose File➤Save as➤PNG.

Fill a Selection with Foreground or Background Color

First, select the foreground or background color you wish to use (see page 2 in this section for instructions). Keep the selection active and press Option-Delete to fill the selection with the foreground color. If you are in the Background layer or any layer that has the Preserve Transparency option turned on, then you can press Delete to fill in the selection with the background color.

You can also fill in your selections by choosing Edit➤Fill.

This causes the Fill dialog box to appear, enabling you to establish the Contents option you wish to use, the Opacity, and the blending Mode.

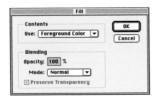

TIP If a selection is empty (a transparent area of a layer) and the Preserve Transparency option is turned on for that layer, you will not be able to fill the selection. To fill the selection, simply turn off the Preserve Transparency option before filling it.

Flatten an Image

To flatten an image (merge all the layers into a single layer), choose Flatten Image from the Layers palette arrow menu, or choose Layer➡Flatten Image.

Load a Selection

Shortcut: Hold down the Command [Control] key and click the channel (on the Channels palette) containing the selection you want to load.

To load a selection, choose Select➡Load Selection. This brings up the Load Selection dialog box, where you can establish document, channel, and operation variables.

17

 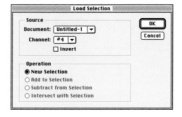

Load a Transparency as a Selection Mask (of a Layer)

To load a layer transparency as a selection mask, hold down the Command [Control] key and click on the thumbnail (on the Layers palette) containing the transparency as a selection mask you want to load.

Make a Channel Active

To make a channel active for editing or modification, click on its thumbnail or title in the Channels palette.

You can tell the channel is active if it is highlighted with a color and its title text becomes bold.

Make a Layer Active

To make a layer active, click on its thumbnail or title in the Layers palette.

You can tell the layer is active if it is highlighted with a color and its title text becomes bold.

Make a Layer Visible/Invisible

To make a Layer visible, click in the leftmost column in the Layers palette. If an eye appears, then the layer is visible. If the column is empty, then that layer is hidden (invisible).

Merge Layer Down

Shortcut: Press Command-E [Control-E].

To merge a Layer down, select the layer and then choose Layer➔Merge Down. Remember to check that the layer you wish to merge down into is visible.

Merge Visible Layers

Shortcut: Press Shift + Command-E [Shift + Control-E].

To merge visible layers, choose Layer➔Merge Visible. See heading Make a layer visible/invisible for a review of how to select layers for merging.

Move a Layer

To move a Layer, click on the layer you want to move in the Layers palette and drag it up or down along the list of layers to the place you want to move it. As you drag the layer, the lines between the layers will darken indicating where the layer will fall if you let go.

The layer you have moved will appear between layers, numerically "out of order."

Return to the Composite Channel

Shortcut: Press Command-~ [Control-~].

If you want to return to the composite channel, click on its thumbnail or title (RGB, CMYK, Lab). The composite channel will always be the one with the Command-~ [Control-~] after its title.

If you are in an RGB file, then channels 0 through 3 should now be active because each of the R, G, and B channels are individual parts of the RGB channel.

Save a File

To save new a file, choose File➡Save. This will bring up the Save dialog box, where you should name your untitled new file and choose a format in which to save it.

To save as another file, choose File➡Save As. This will bring up the Save As dialog box, where you should rename your file and choose a format in which to save it. If a file format which you would like to use is not an option, then use the save a copy command instead.

File format selection is going to depend on what you have in your file, what you want to keep when you save it, and what you're going to do with it afterward. Consult a detailed Web site design book, such as *Creating Killer Web Sites* by David Siegel or *Designing Web Graphics* by Lynda Weinman, for more guidance on which file format is best for your needs.

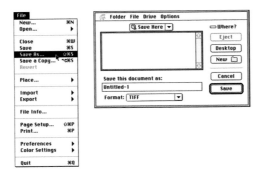

Save as JPEG

To save as a JPEG file format follow the instructions in Save as a file. In the JPEG dialog box, experiment with the JPEG settings to find the best result for each photograph. Set the options to maximize image quality while keeping the file size as small as possible.

JPEG (Joint Photographic Experts Group) has become the standard for displaying photographs and other continuous tone images on the Web. The JPEG is a lossy compression routine that reduces file sizes without reducing color depth (JPEG supports millions of colors). Because JPEG is a lossy technique, don't resave a JPEG format again as a JPEG. The image will deteriorate.

Photoshop Web Magic

Save a Selection

Shortcut: Click on the save selection icon on the Channels palette.

To save a selection, choose Select➔Save Selection.

The Save Selection dialog will open. Choose your desired options and click OK to save the selection.

Switch Foreground/Background Colors

Shortcut: Press X to switch the foreground and background colors.

To switch the foreground and background colors, click on the Switch Colors icon. This flips the two colors shown in this icon only, and does not affect the image.

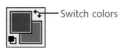

Switch colors

Switch to Default Colors

Shortcut: Press D to switch to the default foreground and background colors.

To change the foreground and background colors to black and white respectively, click on the Default Colors icon.

Default colors

PART I

Backgrounds

The background's "look and feel" sets the stylistic foundation for your Web site. You can select either a solid color or a texture for a background. Solid colors are assigned as hex color values using the body color command in HTML. For textured backgrounds, GIFs or JPEGs can be used. On a Web page, the browser tiles the background image. To create faster download times, make your tiles small—about 96×96 pixels.

There is, of course, no 100 percent performance guarantee when downloading any file from the Web. When assigning textured backgrounds to your Web pages, also choose a background color for your default that is the dominant color in your texture. If there is a technical glitch and the textured look does not download correctly, then your default background color is visible. The Web site design still looks great.

When writing the HTML body background command, make sure that the color command comes first before assigning the JPEG or GIF background texture file. Whatever is assigned last is the look the browser will display.

Patterns on Web page background tiles can be matched on all sides creating a totally seamless background image. By using Photoshop's offset filter you can make your own patterns tile seamlessly.

1 Create a new file. It can be any size, but should be square. Later you will reduce it to the actual size of the tile.

2 Choose Filter➡Texture➡ Texturizer (Sandstone, Scaling: 100%, Relief: 8%). This filter makes it a snap to create basic textures (brick, burlap, canvas, and sandstone) for your backgrounds.

3 Create a new layer (Layer 1). Double-click the Line tool icon on the Toolbox to view the Line tool palette (Opacity: 100%, Line Width: 2, Anti-aliased on, Arrowheads: At Start). Draw a few lines to create a random pattern. Keep the lines toward the right side and bottom of the image so the offset filter will work.

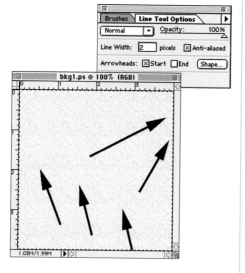

24

4 Select➤All. Choose Filter➤
Other➤Offset (Horizontal: 80
pixels right, Vertical: 80 pixels
down, Undefined Areas: Wrap
Around). This filter wraps one
side of the image around to the
opposite side.

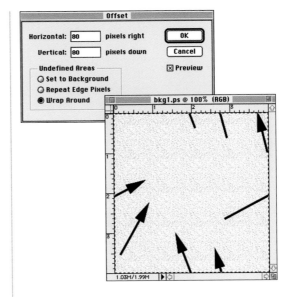

5 With the Line tool, fill in the
empty spaces.

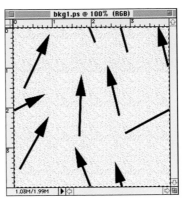

6 Adjust the opacity of Layer 1 to
20%, using the slider on the
Layers palette.

 **For best results adjust the
opacity to a low setting so
that your pattern does not
interfere with the legibility of
the text on your Web page.**

25

7 Choose Image➤Image Size➤Pixel Dimensions (Width: 72, Height: 72).

TIP To preview your tiled image, select the entire tile and choose Edit➤Define Pattern. Then create a new, larger file, and Edit➤Fill (Pattern).

8 Export to GIF format.

VARIATIONS

1 Instead of the Texturizer filter, we used Photoshop 4.0's Note Paper filter, Filter➤Sketch➤Note Paper (Image Balance: 25, Graininess: 13, Relief: 14).

26

2 Synstelien Design's Dreamtime dingbat font adds the graphic elements.

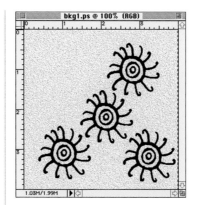

3 The Offset filter moves the dingbats 144 pixels (50% of the image size) to the right and down.

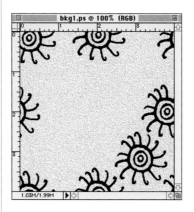

4 We filled in the center of the tile with more dingbats.

5 We flattened the image, chose a foreground color and filled it with (Foreground Color, Opacity: 100%, Mode: Soft Light)

6 Export to GIF format. ■

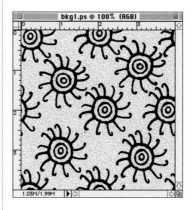

27

Parquet Tiles

You can create interesting and varied parquet effects by rotating and placing tiles within tiles.

1 Open a file containing a texture of your choice or use the granite texture file from the CD (in the textures folder or directory). In this exercise we worked with a 4"×4" file at 72 dpi.

2 Select➔All and copy and paste the image. Choose Layer➔Transform➔Numeric (Scale: Width: 50%, Height: 50%, Rotate: 45°).

3 Choose Filter➔Stylize➔Emboss (Angle: 135, Height: 2 pixels, Amount 50%).

TOOLBOX

Alien Skin's Swirl

Alien Skin's Drop Shadow

4 Choose Image➡Adjust➡Brightness/Contrast (Brightness: 10, Contrast: -5). This makes the inset tile more prominent.

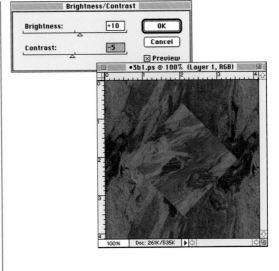

5 Make the Background layer active. To add color to the Background, choose Image➡Adjust➡Variations. We chose to add more yellow.

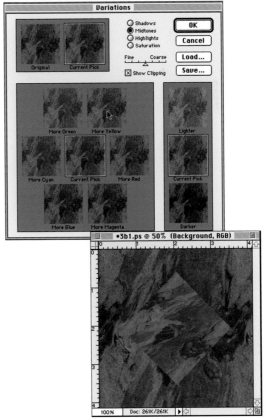

29

6 Make Layer 1 active. Choose Image➔Adjust➔Variations. Drag the Saturation slider up one notch toward Coarse and add yellow.

Offset

Horizontal: 144	pixels right	OK
Vertical: 144	pixels down	Cancel

Undefined Areas

☐ Preview

○ Set to Background
○ Repeat Edge Pixels
◉ Wrap Around

7 Flatten image. Select➔All. Choose Filter➔Other➔Offset (Horizontal: 144, Vertical: 144, Undefined Areas: Wrap Around). The dimensions entered in the Horizontal and Vertical text entry boxes should be 50% of the size of your image, otherwise your image will not wrap correctly.

Brushes **Rubber Stamp Options**

Normal ▾ Opacity: 66%

Option: Clone (non-aligned) ▾

Stylus Pressure: ☐ Size ☐ Opacity

☐ Sample Merged

Brushes Options

35 45 65 100

8 To touch up any hard seams use the Rubber Stamp tool (Opacity: 66%, Clone (non-aligned)). Choose a small- to medium-size soft brush and stroke in the direction of the pattern.

9 Choose Window➾Navigator palette. Use the Navigator palette to zoom into the image for precise cloning. Photoshop 4.0's new Navigator palette enables you to zoom into specific areas using a zoom slider or typing in numeric percentages.

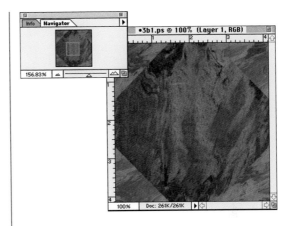

TIP You can also zoom into your image by typing in a new percentage in the lower-left side of your image window.

10 Select Image➾Image Size (Print Size: 50% or smaller, Contains Proportions: On). This resizes the image to create the final tile.

To finish this Web page we made buttons using Alien Skin's Swirl filter and added a drop shadow to define and add depth to the page.

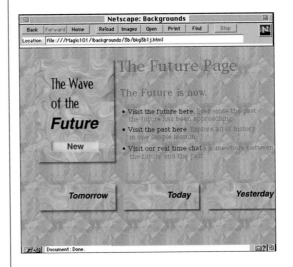

31

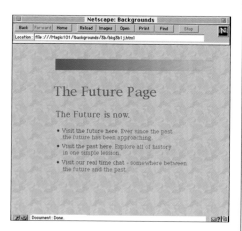

After Step 2, we copied and pasted Layer 1, then rotated it another 45° to create the star pattern. ■

Wave Backgrounds

The ancient art of weaving can be updated for Web pages using Photoshop's Wave filter as a digital loom. With the Wave filter's random function, no two backgrounds are ever quite the same.

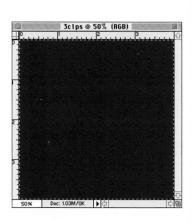

1 Create a new file. Choose white as the foreground color and a dark color for the background color. We used a dark blue in this example. Select➔All and press the Delete key to fill the image with the background color.

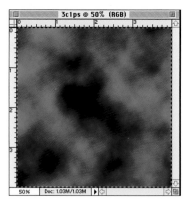

2 Choose Filter➔Render➔Difference Clouds.

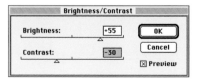

3 Choose Image➔Adjust➔Brightness/Contrast. Move the Brightness slider up to around +55, and the Contrast slider down to around -30. This creates a more even image with less contrast.

The Brightness/Contrast filter can be used on almost any image to lower the contrast so that the pattern does not interfere with the legibility of type on the Web page.

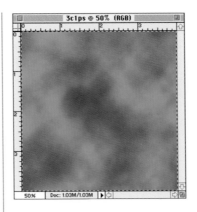

4 Choose Filter➔Distort➔Wave. We used the following settings: Number of Generators: 2; Type: Square; Wavelength: Min: 10, Max: 120; Amplitude: 22: 140; Undefined Areas: Repeat Edge Pixels. Because this filter uses a Randomize function, no two patterns are ever identical. Click the Randomize button until you find a pattern you like.

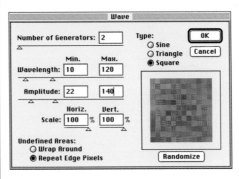

5 Select an area of the image that is evenly blended. This will become the tile.

6 Copy your selection and paste into a new file, then export to GIF format.

VARIATIONS

You can create unlimited patterns by choosing different background colors and randomizing the Wave filter. We kept all other settings the same for this example.

Changing the Number of Generators from 2 to 1 creates larger patterns. ■

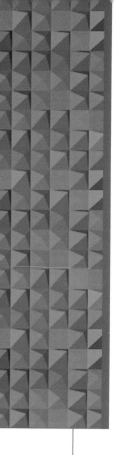

Tiles on Tiles

Photoshop's filters can be used to create quick and easy tiles that are composed of smaller tiles.

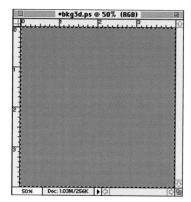

1 Create a new file, choose a background color, and fill the selection with the background color.

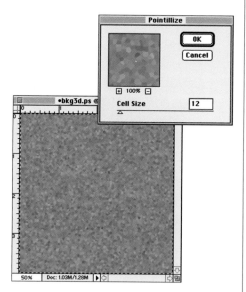

2 Choose Filter➺Pixelate➺ Pointillize (Cell Size: 12).

3 Next, apply Filter➡Stylize➡ Extrude (Type: Pyramids, Size: 20 Pixels, Depth: 8, Random). A smaller size creates smaller tiles.

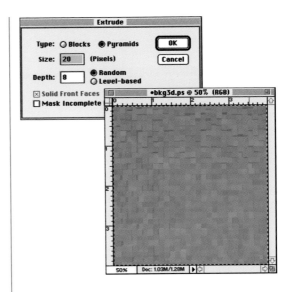

4 Select an area of the image that is fully randomized. Copy and paste the selection to a new file. Save as a JPEG.

We have found that for this image, JPEG files are smaller than GIFs.

39

For this variation, first we removed the color with Image➡Adjust➡Desaturate. The tiles can now be retinted with Image➡Adjust➡Hue Saturation. Click the Colorize checkbox and lower the Saturation to around 50% before selecting your color.

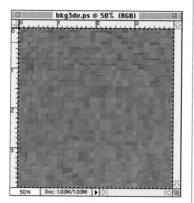

Blocks

For this variation we chose a turquoise color and selected Blocks instead of Pyramids and Solid Front Faces in the Extrude dialog box.

Patchwork

An alternative to the Extrude filter is the Patchwork filter, which creates more uniform squares than the Extrude filter. After Step 2, we applied Filter➞Texture➞Patchwork (Tile Size: 2, Relief: 1).

 For more variations with tiles, try applying additional filters such as Texturizer, Glowing Edges, or Diffuse. ■

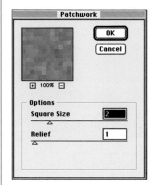

Tiling Photos

Backgrounds made from photographic patterns are a great way to liven up a Web page. Although you might not want to use a photographic background on every page in a site, they can help to identify a page as unique topic or section placemarkers.

1 Open the image for your background tile. The best images for tiles contain repeating or random patterns. We used an image from Photo 24 in this exercise. (This image can be found in the WebMagic folder on the CD.)

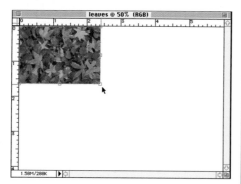

2 Select➔All, then use Layer➔Transform➔Scale to shrink the image to the size you want. Press the Shift key while scaling the image to keep the proportions from changing.

3 Crop the final selection to size by selecting Image➔Crop. After changing an image size or cropping, to sharpen the image always choose Filter➔Sharpen➔Unsharp Mask (we used: Amount: 50, Radius: 1, Threshold: 1). These settings will vary depending upon the image.

4 Choose Image➡Adjust➡Brightness/Contrast to adjust the contrast. For this photograph we set Brightness to +70 and Contrast to -70.

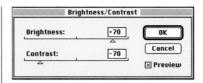

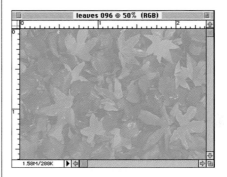

5 Save as JPEG. This file is only 3K when saved as a JPEG; the same GIF file is 16K—a very substantial difference.

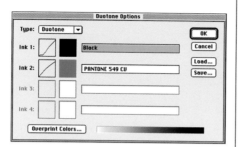

Variations

To make this background more subtle, we removed the color with Image➧Mode➧Grayscale. Then we converted the image to duotone using Image➧Mode➧Duotone. We used black as our first color and green for our second color.

Light-colored type on dark backgrounds can be very effective.

1 Open a file containing a small random pattern, such as this image of coffee beans on a platter.

2 Zoom in to the image and select an area that is random, without any distinguishing characteristics.

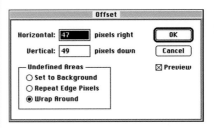

3 Choose Image➥Crop to crop the image to the selection. Then choose Filter➥Other➥Offset about 50% of the image size. In this case we used Horizontal: 47 pixels right, Vertical: 49 pixels down.

45

4 Double-click the Smudge tool icon. Set the Smudge tool Pressure to around 70% and select a small soft brush to work with. Zoom into the image again if you need to and carefully smudge the image across the seam. Use short strokes and follow the direction of the pattern.

5 Save as a JPEG file.

6 Here we choose Image➛ Adjust➛Brightness/Contrast (Brightness: -20, Contrast: -75) to make help make Web page type more legible. ■

Type Wallpaper

Repeating type as a background wallpaper is a common technique used in television news broadcasts and corporate presentations. If you really want to stress the name of the company, Web site, or product, this technique might be just what the doctor ordered.

1 Create a new file and create a new layer. With the Type tool enter the text. Repeat the same word on three lines, once on the first and third lines, twice on the center line, leaving a space between the two words on the center line. Set Text Alignment to Center.

2 This step requires some accuracy. Use the marquee tool to select the top two lines of text (the bottom line of text is used only as a guide for spacing). Begin the selection directly above the bottom line and extend the selection to the top edge of the first line. Letters can be cut through at the ends of the selection as long as both ends of the selection cut through the same letter at the same place.

TIP This exercise is easier to set-up if you use all upper case letters with a font like Helvetica Black or another heavy, sans serif font. When making the marquee selection, leave a small space in front and behind the top word, to insure that the words do not run together when the pattern is applied.

48

3 Save the selection as a new channel (Channel #4) and choose Edit➔Define Pattern.

4 To test if your selection will work as a tile, create a new file and choose Edit➔Fill (Use: Pattern, Opacity: 100%, Mode: Normal).

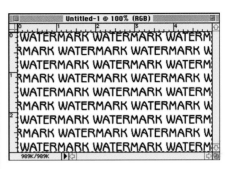

5 Return to the original file. With the type layer selected, set the Opacity slider bar on the Layer palette to 10%. Load the selection Channel #4 Image➔Crop, and use the Unsharp mask Filter➔ Sharpen➔Unsharp Mask to resharpen the image (the unsharp mask settings will vary depending upon your image and the amount of resizing you have done).

6 Export to GIF format.

VARIATIONS

In this example, after Step 2, save the text selection (Channel #4). Select➔All, and fill with the color of your choice. Load the selection Channel #4. Finally, use Image➔ Adjust➔Brightness/Contrast to brighten the selection by setting Saturation to +10%.

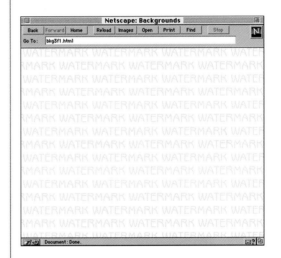

49

TIP To hide the marquee while working use Command-H [Control-H]. This toggles the marquee between visible and invisible while still keeping it active.

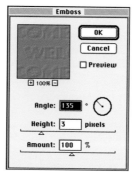

After Step 2, merge layers. Select➤All, then choose Filter➤Stylize➤Emboss (Height 5 pixels, Amount: 100%). Color can be added using Edit➤Fill (Soft Light, 100%). ■

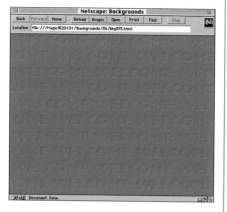

PostScript Patterns

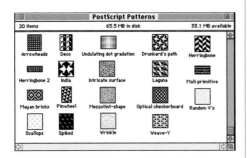

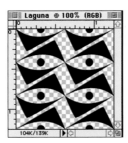

Included with Photoshop is a collection of PostScript Patterns that you can easily use as background tiles in your Web pages. The PostScript Pattern folder is located in the Goodies folder supplied with Photoshop. Our favorite patterns include Deco, Drunkard's path, Laguna, and Optical checkerboard.

1 Open a pattern from the PostScript Patterns folder: Choose File➡Open (Photoshop/ Goodies/Brushes & Patterns/ PostScript Patterns).The postscript patterns will open in Grayscale mode, convert mode to RGB. Note: The Postscript patterns in the Goodies folder are in Adobe Illustrator format—for more information on working with Illustrator files in Photoshop refer to the Photoshop manual.

TIP Illustrator files can be opened at larger sizes or higher resolutions because they are vector-based and therefore resolution independent. Increase the dimensions of the image to create larger tiles.

2 Choose Select➛Color Range (Select: Highlights, Selection Preview: Black Matte, Selection Radio Button chosen). Save the selection (Channel #4)

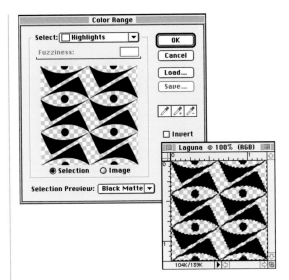

3 Choose Image: Mode (RGB). Choose a foreground color. Select➛All, then choose Edit➛Fill (Use: Foreground Color). (We used RGB values 204, 153, 204). Next, load Channel #4 and fill it with a complementary color.

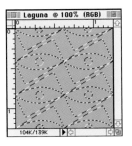

4 Export to GIF format. Because this file uses only two colors, it reduces to around 1K as a GIF.

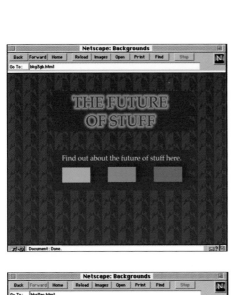

An example of the Deco pattern: Note how contrast has been kept low so that the background does not interfere with legibility of type on the Web page.

To create just a hint of the Scallops pattern on this page we used Filter➤Brightness/Contrast (Brightness: +30, Contrast: -70).

54

To colorize the Mali primitive we chose Image➤Mode (RGB), selected all, and then filled it with soft light, Edit➤Fill (Use: Foreground Color, Opacity: 100%, Mode: Soft Light). ■

Diagonals work nicely as backgrounds for Web pages because they seem to defy the horizontal and vertical tiling of background patterns and they can create interesting effects, (especially wide diagonals) when you are scrolling the page.

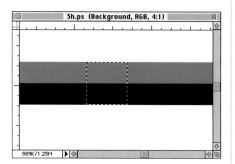

1 Create a new file, and then double-click the Line tool icon on the Toolbox to open the Line tool Options dialog box. Set the line width to 10 pixels and turn anti-aliasing off. Switch to the default colors and draw a black line across the image. Choose a new foreground color, then draw the second line a few pixels away from the first line. Use the Magic Wand tool to select the second line.

2 Zoom into the page to enlarge the image, and with the line selected choose the Move tool and use the arrow key to move the line so they both touch. Then use the rectangular Marquee tool to select a portion of both lines from top to bottom.

56

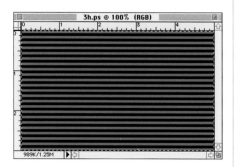

3 Choose Edit➤Define Pattern. Select all and choose Edit➤Fill (Pattern, 100%, Normal).

For color consistency across platforms use the non-dithering 216 color palette for fill colors in your backgrounds.

4 With the image still selected, choose Image➧Rotate Canvas➧ Arbitrary (Angle: 45% CCW).

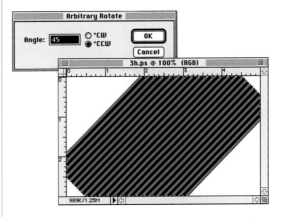

5 Zoom into the image again to make the selection for the tile. Choose an even number of stripes, begin with the top left corner on a black stripe and end with the bottom right corner just touching a black line. Keep the selection square by holding down the Shift key while dragging. Save the selection (Channel #4).

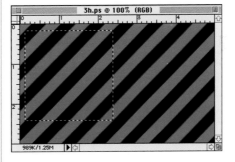

6 Copy and paste the selection into a new file and export to GIF format.

57

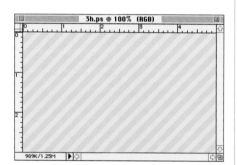

1 After Step 5, choose Select➝Color Range (Select: Sampled Colors, Fuzziness: 80, Selection Preview: None, and choose Selection). Press the cursor on a black line and then click OK. All the black in your image should now be selected. Save this selection (Channel #5).

2 To create subtle lines first select all and press Delete. Load the selection Channel #5 and choose Image➝Adjust➝Brightness/Contrast (Brightness: +10, Contrast: 0)

3 Choose Select➝Inverse then Select➝Feather (Radius: 3 pixels) and then Image➝Brightness/Contrast (Brightness: -60, Contrast: 0). This adds some dimension to the stripes.

58

Fabric Textures

The Glowing Edges filter was applied next to create this fabric-like texture. Select Filter➔Stylize➔ Glowing Edges (Edge Width: 4, Edge Brightness: 6, Smoothness: 1). ■

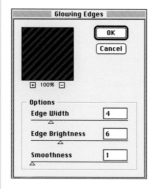

Borders

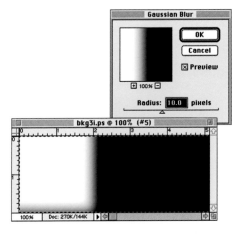

1 Create a new file at least 640 pixels wide—the minimum width of a standard computer monitor. When creating background graphics with a border, note that the tile should run the full width of the screen. Choose View➤Show Grid and select an area about 2 inches wide on the left side of the image, save the selection (Channel #4), and then fill it with the color of your choice. Choose View➤ Hide Grid.

2 To make a drop shadow on the border, duplicate Channel #4 (Channel #5). Then make Channel #5 visible. Choose Filter➤Blur➤ Gaussian Blur (Radius: 10.0 pixels). Leaving Channel #5 selected, hold down the Option [Alt] key and press the right arrow key twice. The result will extend the drop shadow by 2 pixels.

TIP Sometimes when creating channel selections that have had a Gaussian Blur applied, the following may appear in a dialog box: "Warning: No pixels are more than 50% selected. The selection edges will not be visible." This is not a problem. Click OK.

3 Return to the composite channel. Load the selection Channel #5, then load the selection Channel #4, but use subtract from selection. Select Edit➡Fill (Use: Black, Opacity 80%).

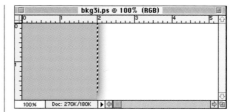

4 Select an area that is the full width of the image and about ½ inch in height. Copy and paste the selection into a new file. Choose Layers➡Flatten Image. Export to GIF format.

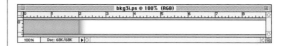

 TIP Large areas of white or a single color do not substantially add to the size of GIF files.

VARIATIONS

To make a background look like note paper, draw two vertical lines for the border and one horizontal line across the image. The height of your selection will equal the line spacing on the background.

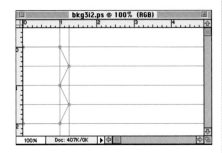

1 Create a new file **640 pixels** wide. Photoshop 4.0's new Guides feature is especially helpful when creating artwork that requires accuracy. Add vertical guides at 1 inch and 1 ¼ inches and five horizontal guides ½ inch apart.

2 Using the Pen tool, draw a path with three hinge points on the left side and two hinge points on the right side. Place the right top, center, and bottom hinge points at 1 inch and place the other two hinge points at 1 ¼ inch.

3 Select the Convert Anchor Point tool from under the Pen tool in the Toolbox. Click the hinge point at 1 ¼ inch and drag down vertically ¼ inch to create a curve point.

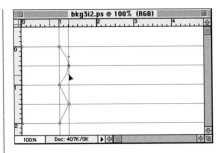

4 Repeat the above step on the second hinge point at 1 ¼ inch. Then double-click the Work Path in the Paths palette to save the path as a selection.

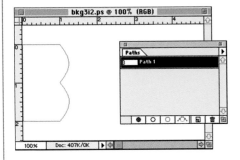

5 Choose a foreground color. From the Paths pop-up menu choose Fill➡Path (Use: Foreground Color). Then use the rectangular Marquee tool to make a selection that includes only one curve in the scallop and is the full width of the image (640 pixels).

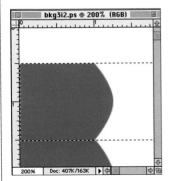

6 Copy and paste the selection into a new file and export to GIF format. ■

Tile Machines

Terazzo

Terazzo is a commercial program by Xaos Tools specifically designed to make tile patterns. Select an image (for this example we choose a stock photo from Photo24 Texture Resource) and move Terrazzo's selection tile around to get instant tileable artwork!

Dragging or resizing the tile creates new patterns.

Terrazo offers 18 different symmetries for creating all kinds of patterns. This is an example of Primrose Path symmetry.

Kai's Power Tools

Kai's Power Tools by MetaTools is one of the most useful and innovative collections of filters made for Photoshop. Texture Explorer is one of the most useful tools you can find for creating new textures from scratch.

If you don't have Texture Explorer, don't fret. You can find a sampling of background tiles made with KPT at the KPT Backgrounds Archive Web page:

```
http://the-tech.mit.edu/
cgibin/KPT_bgs2.pl?Orig
inal1. ■
```

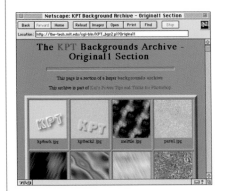

PART II

Titling

If there is one thing that can truly define the visual style and identity of a Web site, it is the application of typography. The choice of font styles, the size and color of the text, and the organization of type on the page create the dominant graphic identity of the site.

Unlike print, the Web page is a dynamic medium. Successfully combining decorative bitmapped type created in Photoshop with HTML-generated fonts requires an understanding and acceptance that the viewer is now your partner in the design process. Your Web page design can and will be modified by the viewer's browser, selected browser preferences, operating system, and hardware configuration.

Large ornamental type is used sparingly as a substitute for photographic images or illustrations. Any type on a Web page that is not HTML-generated text is bitmapped and viewed at screen resolution, either at 72 or 100 dpi. To maximize text readability use a solid-colored, anti-aliased typeface.

When you select the 216-color safe palette (also called a non-dithering palette), your smaller text will not lose legibility when viewed across different computer platforms. The safe palette works well because the colors are not dithered. Dithered colors don't work because they are visual simulations of color, just like a pointillist painting. A dithered color, built by selecting pixels from the available colors in a palette, is a random pattern your eye optically reads as a solid color. Filling text with a dithered color pattern adds visual noise to the font. This noise causes the thin strokes of the characters and smaller-sized text to lose image clarity.

Shadows for Buttons

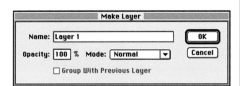

Make Layer

Name: Layer 1   OK

Opacity: 100 % Mode: Normal ▾   Cancel

☐ Group With Previous Layer

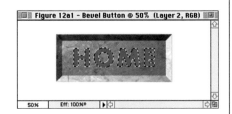

Figure 12a1 – Bevel Button @ 50% (Layer 2, RGB)

HOME

50%   Eff: 100%°   ▶ ◇

Shadowed text works well in buttons with textures by helping to demarcate the text from the button. Adding a black shadow to the text helps to sharpen the edge of the letters, making them easier to read.

1 Create a new file with mode set to RGB and background transparent, or open a file containing the selected button style. We are using Bevel button on page 126.

2 In layers dialog box, double-click background to open make layer dialog box. Rename background: Layer 1. Choose a foreground color for your label, maximizing contrast of foreground to background.

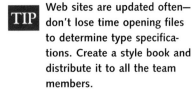

TIP If you open a file that has been flattened, there will only be a Background. Renaming the background as Layer 1 creates a transparent background.

3 Enter the text. We selected Futura Bold, center alignment, anti-aliased on, spacing: 3. Use the move tool to position the text. This is Layer 2.

TIP Web sites are updated often—don't lose time opening files to determine type specifications. Create a style book and distribute it to all the team members.

4 Duplicate Layer 2 and name it Layer 3. Move Layer 3 below Layer 2. Make the Layer 2 invisible. Select Layer 3 shadow text. Choose Edit➟Fill (Use Black).

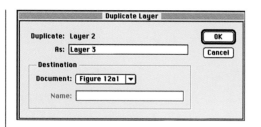

5 Choose Filter➟Gaussian Blur (1 pixel). A slight blur makes the shadow appear to be part of the button's surface.

6 Select the Move tool. Using the arrow keys, move the shadow 4 pixels to the left and 4 pixels up. The Shadow should not appear to be touching the next character in Layer 2 text.

7 Layer 2 visible again and keep the Layer 3 active. Check for legibility of text. Adjust the postioning of shadow to foreground text as needed. Deselect the shadow.

8 Export GIF format.

VARIATION

You can create the effect of light hitting the text and creating the shadow. Using the Eyedropper tool, choose a light foreground color from the button texture to color match text highlight to the button color palette. Repeat Steps 4 and 5. Rename the layer as Layer 4. Move Layer 4 below Layer 2, but above the Shadow. Move the highlight text one pixel horizontally, and vertically one pixel to the side opposite the drop shadow. ∎

Object Shadows

Use drop shadows in your Web pages to help identify graphics and artwork that function as clickable links. This helps people to visually identify and separate the different elements of the page.

Here we used a variety of third-party plug-in filters to create different kinds of shadow effects. Check out the demos and sample catalog on the CD-ROM. (An optional Photoshop filter to use instead will appear between brackets.)

1 Open a file containing the image or texture you want to use. Select one from the MetaTools Power Photos Series sampler collection included on the CD-ROM.

2 Create a new file.

©PhotoSpin 1995

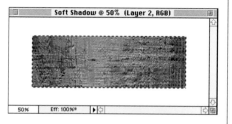
Soft Shadow @ 50% (Layer 2, RGB)
50%   Eff: 100%

3 Select a rectangular area with the Marquee tool large enough to fit your text with a shadow. Edit➤Paste into Paste your previously copied image into the selection, creating a new layer with a layer mask.

4 In Layer 2, use the Marquee tool to select the rectangle selection that you pasted into. To soften the wood grain texture, choose Filter➤Blur➤KPT Gaussian Blur Weave [Angled Strokes].

72

TOOLBOX

Alien Skin's
Drop Shadow
Motion Trail
Carve

KPT Gaussian
Blur Weave
Electricity

5 Remove the layer mask by dragging the Layer Mask icon into the Trash icon on the Layers palette. Press the Apply button when the Warning dialog box appears.

 When you drag the Layer Mask into the Trash, a dialog box appears giving you the option to discard or apply the mask. If you apply the mask all unused areas of the image hidden by the Mask are removed.

6 Using the rectangular Marquee tool, select the textured rectangle and add an Alien Skin Black Box Drop Shadow (X and Y shadow Offset 32 pixels, Blur 25, Opacity 60%, Shadow Color black).

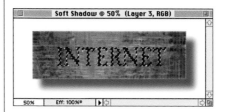

7 Create a new layer (Layer 3). Use the Eyedropper tool to select a dark gray color from the textured image for the foreground color. Select the Type tool and enter the text (center alignment).

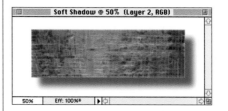

8 Duplicate Layer 3 twice (changing the name to Layer 4 and Layer 5). Make Layer 3 active and make Layers 4 and 5 invisible.

9 Use the Magic Wand tool to select Layer 3 text. Choose Filter➛Blur➛KPT Gaussian Electrify [Gaussian Blur]. Select the Move tool and use the arrow keys to move the text 7 pixels right and 7 pixels down. Deselect text.

73

10 Make Layer 4 visible and active. Make Layer 3 invisible. With the Magic Wand tool and Shift key, select the text on Layer 4. Fill the selection with a new foreground color. We used a medium blue, (15, 72, 149) for this example.

11 Choose Filter➡Alien Skin➡ Motion Trail (length 24 pixels, opacity 80%, direction 315°, with Just Smear Edges activated) [Wind].

12 Make Layer 5 visible. Choose a foreground color (we used 231, 213, 214) With the Magic Wand tool, select the text and fill with the light beige color.

13 Export the image to GIF format.

TIP The Paste into command adds layers. To keep file sizes manageable, merge down layers wherever possible. ■

Filling Type with an Image

Pasting an image into a heading maximizes use of screen area. By combining pictures with text, the enhanced effect adds both decorative value and visual meaning to the words. This technique can be particularly useful for Web sites targeting an international, multi-linguistic audience.

1 Open the PhotoDisc image file or another stock photograph that complements your Web page design.

© PhotoDisc, Inc. 1996

Image Size		

Pixel Dimensions: 298K (was 10.1M)

Width: 282 | pixels
Height: 360 | pixels

OK
Cancel
Auto...

Print Size:

Width: 3.921 | inches
Height: 5 | inches
Resolution: 72 | pixels/inch

☒ Constrain Proportions
☒ Resample Image | Bicubic

2 Choose Image➞Image Size and totally resize the image to fit the design layout (in our example, 3.5 inches by 3.5 inches, 72 dpi). Choose Filter➞Sharpen➞Unsharp Mask.

TIP Avoid converting a high resolution 300 dpi image directly to 72 dpi. It is better to make the transition in several steps using 300, 266, 200 and 72 dpi. (These numbers and steps may vary: Factor in image content and detail. Test

76

different settings and compare results. Save the settings for future reference.)

Apply the Unsharp Mask to the final file. However, remember when applying unsharp mask settings, what you see onscreen is what you will want to use in your Web page. Begin with a threshold setting of five for images with skin tones.

3 Create a new file. Enter the text using the Type Mask tool. We selected Franklin Gothic Heavy (center alignment).

4 Copy the resampled image and Edit➤Paste Into the type selection and enable the layer mask. Apply, then remove, the layer mask. This masks out unused portions of the image.

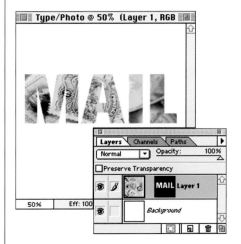

77

5 Create a drop shadow with the Alien Skin Black Box filter. Filter settings are x shadow offset: 7 pixels, y shadow offset: 9 pixels, blur: 61, opacity: 88% and shadow color: black. If you don't have the Alien Skin filter, see Shadows (page 70) for an alternative method. Deselect the text. Fill the background with a color. Save.

VARIATIONS

Adding a Selection

1 Open another PhotoDisc image—an envelope, located in the PhotoDisc folder on the CD-ROM. Repeat Step 2. Use the Pen tool to select the envelope. This creates a Work Path in the Paths palette.

 © PhotoDisc, Inc. 1996

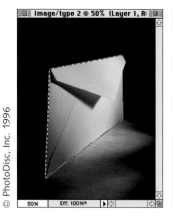

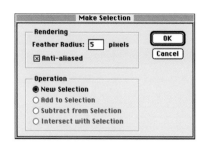

2 In the Path palette pop-up menu, choose Make Selection (Feather: 5 pixels).

3 Copy and Paste the selected envelope into the new file with the text and background. Move Layer 2 below Layer 1.

4 Select Layer 1. Use the Move tool to reposition the text to the bottom of the window. Save as a new file.

5 Export to GIF format. ■

3D Type

For text heavy sites, translating a 2D header or label into three-dimensional letters can easily bring a distinctive, one-of-a-kind look to your Web page. Animated 3D "flying logos," like those seen in the opening titling sequence of a TV program, can add visual interest and create an easy to remember identity for your Web site or corporate banner. If you are interested in animating your 3D type, check out our Animation section beginning on page 205.

If you would like to add 3D type or icons to your Web page, but you don't know how to do 3D graphics—here is an alternative. Using the Photoshop Type Mask tool, one-color decorative fonts can be filled with different colors, tones, and textures to create a simulated 3D effect.

1 Create a new file or open a file containing the selected button style. We are using Bevel Button on page 126.

2 Choose Image➡Rotate Canvas➡ 180°. Rotating the canvas will make the button's light source match the shadow pattern on the text.

80

3 Choose Image➞Adjust➞ Hue/Saturation. Adjust the hue slider bar to +85 to create a green button.

4 Duplicate the background layer and rename it Type. Hide the background layer.

5 Make the Type layer active and use the Type Mask tool to enter the text. We selected BuxomD (center alignment and Spacing: 3). If you don't have BuxomD, we provide a file, 3Dtype, with the word HOME typeset in the CD-ROM folder named WebMagic. You can use the file to create a mask.

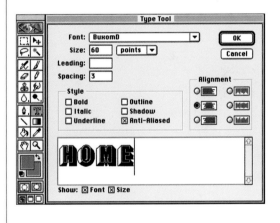

81

TIP	To select and move individual characters in a type mask, use Quick Mask mode or a channel.

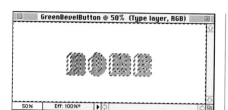

GreenBevelButton @ 50% (Type layer, RGB)

50%   Eff: 100%*

6 Invert the type mask. Choose Select➛Inverse and delete. The Type layer displays filled text with a transparent background.

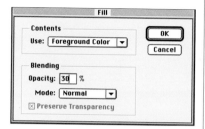

Fill

Contents
Use: Foreground Color ▾

OK
Cancel

Blending
Opacity: 30 %
Mode: Normal ▾
☒ Preserve Transparency

7 Choose Select➛Inverse. Keep the type mask active. Edit➛Fill (Use: Black, Opacity: 30%). This darkens the textured text to match the button's right side bevel.

Gaussian Blur

OK
Cancel
☒ Preview

⊞ 100% ⊟

Radius: 2.0 pixels

8 Choose Filter➛Gaussian Blur (2 pixels). Make the background color visible. The type and button now appear to be molded together. Deselect the text.

GreenBevelButton @ 50% (Background, RGB)

50%   Eff: 94%*

9 Make the background layer active. Use the Marquee tool to select the left button bevel. Choose Edit➛Copy. We are copying the button's left bevel to paste into the left side of each letter.

GreenBevelButton @ 50% (Layer 4, RGB)

50%   Eff: 100%*

10 Select the Type layer. Use the Magic Wand tool to select the left side of each letter one at a time. Choose Edit➛Paste Into, pasting in the section of the bevel you copied in Step 9. Paste into creates a layer mask. Remove the layer mask by dragging the Layer Mask icon into the Trash icon on the Layers palette. Deselect the text.

11 Use the Magic Wand tool and the shift key to select the top face of each letter. Fill the selection with the foreground color. (We used the RGB values 39, 17, 46.) Deselect the text.

12 Use the Magic Wand tool and the Shift key to select the shadow in each letter. Choose Select➤ Inverse. Enter Quick Mask. Edit the mask to deselect all areas except lower portions of letters and the base of letter E's three horizontal cross-strokes. Exit Quick Mask.

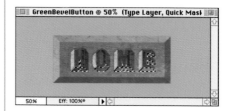

13 Choose Edit➤Fill. (Use: Black, Opacity: 30%) to fill the selection with black.

14 Export to GIF format. ■

OUTLINE CAPS

TOOLBOX

KPT Texture
Explorer

Outlined Caps

When pictures are not appropriate, substitute large numbers as decorative elements on a Web page. Numbers can help organize information and they also serve as imagemaps to "hot link" to other pages or Web sites.

1 Create a new file. Keep file dimensions (height and width) to a minimum. Set margins as narrow as possible to keep files small for faster file download times.

2 Choose a foreground color to be the outline color. We picked a bright yellow (RGB 251, 243, 5). Enter the text. We used Futura Extra Black (center alignment). With the Magic Wand tool, select number 8. Use the Move tool to move it into position. Keep the text selected.

3 Turn off the Preserve Transparency Option. Choose Edit➔Stroke (8 pixels) to convert the text to outline font. The text has a yellow stroke and a yellow fill. Press Delete to remove the yellow fill.

4 Duplicate Layer 1 twice. Rename Layer 1 copies: Layer 2 and Layer 3. Hide Layer 3. Make Layer 2 active. Because we will apply a Gaussian blur to the yellow outline, we created this second duplicate layer to keep a copy of the colored line at full intensity and sharpness.

5 Choose Filter➤Gaussian Blur (2 pixels).

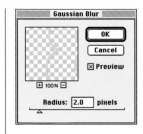

TIP If you want a larger glow around your letter, try Filter➤ Stylize➤Glowing Edges or the Alien Skin Black Box filter Glow.

6 Select Layer 1. Use the magic wand tool to select the interior space between the outlines of the unblurred number 8 on Layer 1. Turn off the preserve transparency option. Choose a foreground color, a vivid green (RGB 18, 140, 53). Fill the selected center area of the letter.

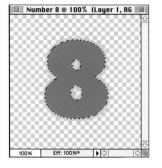

7 With the center of the letter still selected, choose Filter➤Noise➤ Add Noise (80 pixels, Distribution Uniform)

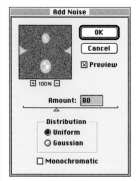

8 Make the Layer 3 visible. Flatten the image. Export to GIF format.

This is a
of copy f
Web Mag
sample bl
for Photo
This is a
of copy f
Web Mag

VARIATIONS

Another alternative is to fill the text with a texture and then crystallize the filled area. Repeat steps 1-6, but apply a texture with a filter instead. (We used Filter➤KPT Texture Explorer 2.1➤Effects textures➤Egyptian Green.) After the text is filled, select Filter➤Pixelate➤Crystallize. Set Cell Size to 10. ∎

Initial Caps

KPT Gradient Designer offers a wide assortment of patterns to create backdrops for initial letters. When reducing file sizes for faster downloads, some gradients may band when used with a limited color palette. As an alternative, an additional filter can be applied to create a hand-drawn effect before the file is exported to GIF or saved as a JPEG file.

The typeface is ITC Rennie Mackintosh Ornaments for each of the following five examples. We provide these five ornaments filled with gradients as preset files on the CD-ROM, in the WebMagic folder. If you would like to try other gradients, check out the KPT Gradient Designer demo on the CD-ROM or select the Photoshop 4.0 Gradient tool.

Ornament A

Open the file CRM1. Select Ornament A. Use Filter➡Blur to remove jaggies. Apply Filter➡Texture➡ Mosaic Tiles

TOOLBOX

KPT Gradient Designer

Xaos Tools
Paint Alchemy

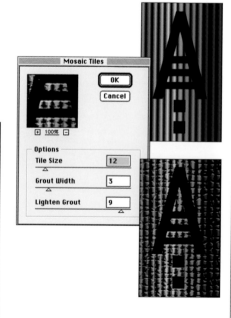

Ornament B

Open the file CRM2. Select Ornament B. Apply Filter➡Brush Strokes➡Spatter. Use the default settings.

Ornament C

Open the file CRM3. Select Ornament C. Apply Filter➡ Texture➡Stained Glass (Change size: 5).

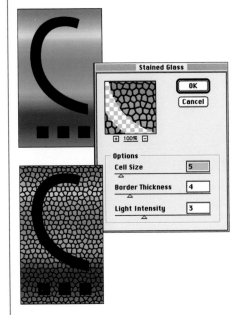

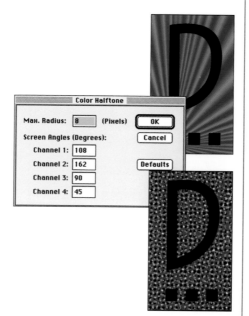

Ornament D

Open the file CRM4. Select Ornament D. Choose Filter➧ Pixelate➧Color Halftone Use default settings.

Ornament E

Open the file CRM5. Select Ornament E. Apply Filter➧Xaos Tools➧Paint Alchemy, with the settings in the dialog box to the left. The Paint Alchemy demo is on the CD-ROM. ■

Free Transform

Adobe has updated the Transform features in Photoshop 4.0. Here we combine Transform—numeric entry with the new Free Transform feature and the Radial Blur and Ripple filters to create warped text on a painterly background.

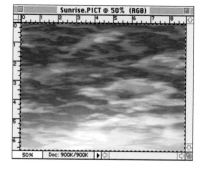

1 Create a new file, or open a file containing a textured background. There are samples in the Adobe folder on the CD-ROM. For this example, we picked Sunrise, created with Adobe TextureMaker.

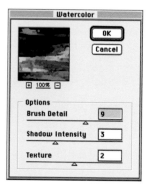

2 Choose Filter➔Artistic➔ Watercolor. (Shadow Intensity: 3, Texture: 2). This filter creates a more painterly and irregular textured effect.

TIP Photoshop 4.0 incorporates the Gallery Effects artistic effects filters that were separate plug-ins for 3.0. They can convert an over used stock photograph into a fresh new look. Experiment with the settings and set-up a library of pre-sets. It will save production time later.

3 Create a new file. Make the stock photo texture file active. Check the pixel dimensions of the file you created in Step 1. In the Marquee Options palette choose Style➥Fixed Size. Enter the pixel dimensions of the Step 1 file. Drag the marquee selection from the stock photo file to the new file. The new file now has the photographic texture as a background on Layer 1.

4 Use the Eyedropper tool to choose a foreground color from the background texture. Enter the text. We selected Helvetica Bold, center alignment, anti-aliased on, spacing: 0. Use the Move tool to position the text. This creates Layer 2.

5 Select the cap "F". Choose Layer➥Transform➥Numeric (Shift-Command-T) [Shift-Control-T] Set Scale to Width: 90%, Height: 100%, Skew to Horizontal and Vertical: -5°.

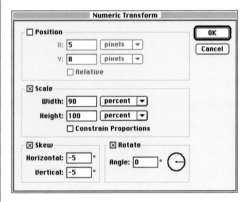

93

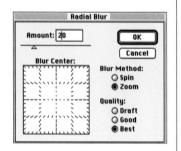

94

6 Repeat the procedure for the lower case "r", and the two "e"s. For each letter we increased the numeric value for scale by 5% for both the height and the width, skew by 2° horizontally and vertically, plus or minus and rotate by 10°. The important factor is to create a fluid visual flow as your eye moves from one letter to another.

7 Select the letters "form". While selected choose Layer➤Free Transform (Command-T) [Control-T]. A selection box with handles will appear. Move the cursor so that it is outside the selection box and rotate the selection clockwise. Use the Escape key to cancel any changes you are not satisfied with.

TIP If the cursor shows a straight line with arrows at each end, you can scale the height or width by moving in a straight line. Moving at a 45° angle to the corner changes both height and width at the same time. If the arrows on the cursor are at an angle to each other, then you will be rotating the selection.

8 Deselect the floating selection and duplicate Layer 2 Hide Layer 2 copy. Select the text on Layer 2. Choose Edit➤Fill (Use: Black). This will be the shadow text. Apply Filter➤Blur➤Radial Blur. Try settings in figure. The blur filter creates a sensation of shimmering motion.

9 While the text on Layer 2 is selected, choose Layer➔ Transform➔Numeric (Shift-Command-T) [Shift-Control-T] and rotate all the text clockwise an additional 15°. This makes the shadow more visible behind the foreground text.

10 Make Layer 2 copy visible, and active. Choose the first three letters and apply Filter➔Distort➔ Ripple (Amount: 100%, Size: Medium).

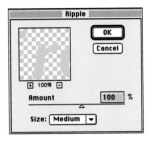

11 Deselect first three letters. Select the remaining five letters. Apply the Ripple filter again, but change the size to large.

12 Export to GIF format. ■

PART III

Icons

Icons and pictographs are popular on Web pages because they transcend language barriers and international borders. Icons quickly identify key elements and links on a Web page.

As informational devices within a site, icons should represent a common visual style and clearly reinforce the literal meaning of the link or page identity, such as "mail" or "home page." You can use icons on buttons to serve as placemarkers that help the site visitor find information. The same icon can then be used as an identifier in a page header to brand that page or section.

Just like fonts, icons are available as collections in a wide variety of themes and styles. Use Photoshop filters, such as Bas Relief or Neon Glow and Photoshop color editing techniques, to customize these icons to fit your personal design style.

A word of caution—before using any stock art collection or trademark, read the small print on the package. Some collections are for print use only, and their licensing agreements forbid distribution via electronic media. Find out what a company's policy is before using its trademarks. Written permission may be required.

2D Clip Art

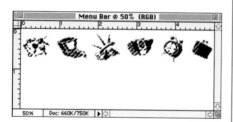

Creating a dramatic menu bar from 2D clip art is fast and easy with Photoshop 4.0. By enhancing and modifying Dingbat fonts you can quickly create a site worthy of a Fortune 500 company.

1 Create a new file. Type your images using a dingbat font or import 2D clip art into your new file. Save the selection (Channel #4). We used the DF Commercials font for this example.

2 Choose foreground and background colors. We chose royal blue for the foreground and white for the background. A white background gives the best results.

TIP You can complement the use of Dingbat and Ornaments fonts in menu bars by also using them as a subtle background pattern. Use pale colors or light gray for background patterns.

3 Select➤None. Choose
Filter➤Sketch➤Bas Relief.

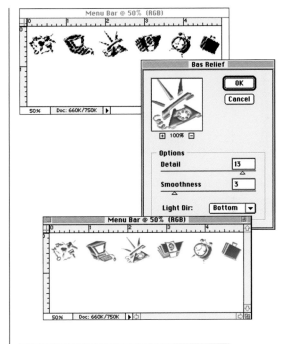

4 Add more dimension to your
button bar by implementing the
drop shadow technique. See
Shadows, page 70, for detailed
instructions.

5 With the Type tool, enter the
text for each button.

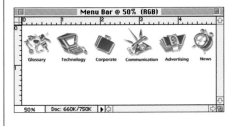

6 With the Crop tool, crop your
final image as close as possible to
ensure fast download. Export to
GIF format.

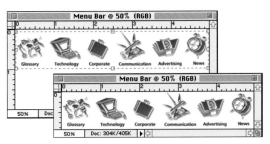

Glossary   Technology   Corporate   Communication   Advertising   News

Brightness/Contrast

Brightness: `+100`   OK

Contrast: `-27`   Cancel

☒ Preview

Glossary   Technology   Corporate   Communication   Advertising   News

VARIATIONS

Adjusting the brightness and contrast creates a subtle, washed-out effect. Load the selection Channel #4 and choose Image➤Adjust➤ Brightness/Contrast (Brightness: +100, Contrast: -27). Try different settings until you find ones that suit your colors and art.

You can also select each clip art icon and vary the Color Balance to create a variety of colors in your menu bar. ∎

Neon

Neon

Just as in real life, a neon sign on a Web page can attract attention to the site.

1 Open a file containing black-and-white line art. For this exercise we used an outline of a typical mail icon. (The icon can be found in the WebMagic folder on the CD). If the image you choose is in gray tone mode, convert mode to RGB.

2 Select the black area of the icon from the original image with the Magic Wand tool. Create a new document 20 pixels larger than the size of the icon. Using the Move tool, drag a copy into the new document. Save the selection (Channel #4). Select➔All and fill the background with black.

3 On the new layer (Layer 1), load a channel selection (Channel #4). Choose Edit➔Fill (Use: White).

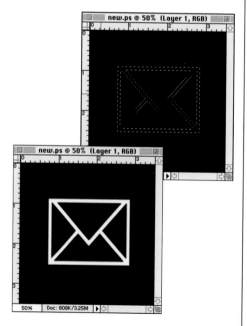

102

4 Choose new foreground and background colors. Use bright colors with different tonal values that will work well together (one light and one dark) making the darker one the background color. In this example we used Pantone 1788 and Pantone 257 respectively. Create a new layer (Layer 2). Select➔Load Selection (#4). Edit➔ Fill (Use: Background Color).

5 Create a new layer (Layer 3), (the selection from Step 2 is now active on the new layer). Edit➔Fill➔(Use: Foreground color).

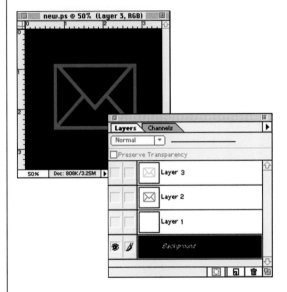

6 Hide Layer 3 and make Layer 2 active and Load the selection Channel #4. Select➔Modify➔ Contract (Width 3 pixels). Delete the selection. The deleted area makes part of Layer 1 visible.

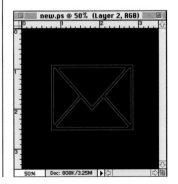

103

7 Make Layer 3 active and load the selection Channel #4. Select➤Modify➤Contract (width 2 pixels) and delete the selection.

8 Make Layer 1 active. Choose Filter➤Blur➤Gaussian Blur (5 pixels). Repeat the process for Layer 2 (3 pixels) and Layer 3 (1.5 pixels.)

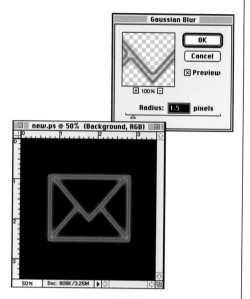

9 Make all layers visible and Save the file as neon1.ps (Photoshop document). Export as a GIF with the name neon1.gif. This will give you the final glowing neon icon.

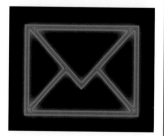

10 To add a flashing effect to this image, Revert to neon.ps. Hide Layer #1 (white) and export as a GIF.

TIP The exported GIFs from your image (neon1.gif and neon2.gif) can be built into an animated GIF image using a GIF animation program, and added to an HTML page for a flashing neon sign effect. ∎

PART IV

Rules

Rules are both decorative and functional elements for organizing Web sites and pages. Rules define columns and page divisions within the compositional grid and highlight areas of content and activity.

On Web pages with large amounts of HTML text, rules act as visual markers helping readers keep their place. Rules, in combination with icons or text links, also serve as navigation options for returning to the top of a page or to other locations in the site.

When selecting a rule style, color, and weight, consider how the rule works with both the HTML text and other graphic devices. Keep things in balance—rules are added detail, not the first thing you notice when looking at a Web page.

Photoshop offers an infinite series of possibilities for creating a library of rules. In the following techniques, we show you how to build rules by customizing brushes or applying filters to Zapf Dingbats. Mix and match. Have fun!

Using Custom Brushes

Horizontal rules are commonly used to divide different categories of information into logical sections. Photoshop's Brush tool can be used to make a wide variety of quick and easy-to-create looks.

1 Create a new file wider than the Web page you are working on. Double-click the Paintbrush tool and select the Brushes tab. Using the palette's pop-up menu, Load Brushes from the Photoshop application's Goodies folder. We loaded the Assorted and the Square brushes.

2 Select the brush shown in the figure. Double-click its icon to access the Brush Options dialog box. Set the Spacing to 150%.

3 Choose a foreground color. Add two vertical guides to define the width of your Web page. Add one horizontal guide as a placement guide.

4 Click at the intersection of the guides on the left side of the image area. Hold the Shift key down and click at the intersection of the guides on the right side of the image area. This draws a line with your paintbrush.

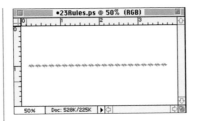

5 As a finishing touch we added a drop shadow. First we used the Magic Wand tool to select the background, inverted the selection, and applied an Alien Skin Drop Shadow. See the Soft Shadow section on page 72 if you don't have the Alien Skin package.

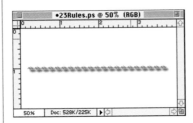

 You can create custom brushes in Photoshop by using part of an image to create the custom brush shape. Choose Define Brush from the Brushes palette menu. For visual clarity and best results the brush should appear on a solid white background.

VARIATIONS

This variation uses square brushes. The red rule was made with the largest brush, with the spacing unaltered at 25%. We set the spacing of the blue rule to 250% and the spacing of the yellow rule to 150%.

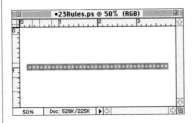

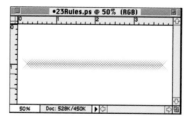

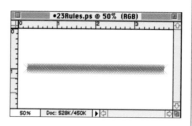

For this variation we combined two brushes to create a mock moiré pattern. The first brush was spaced at 20%; the second at 90%. ■

Using Decorative Fonts

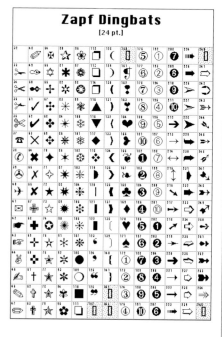

Ornamental and dingbat fonts can be used as a quick and easy way to create original and decorative rules. There are literally thousands of pictograms and embellishments suitable for use in creating rules. In this exercise we used Zapf Dingbats, which is universally available and comes with most computers and many font collections.

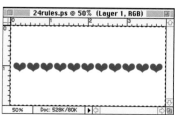

1 Create a new file that is longer than the width of the Web page you are working on. Choose a foreground color. With the Type tool create a row of dingbats (Layer 1). We chose a heart for this rule.

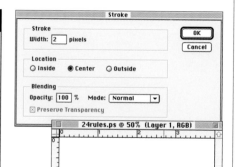

2 Choose a new foreground color (red) and choose Edit➔Stroke (2 pixels, center). This creates a little more visual interest for the rule.

TOOLBOX

Alien Skin's
Cutout

3 As a finishing touch we added a cut-out effect. Duplicate Layer 1 and hide that created layer, Layer 1 copy. Make Layer 1 active and use the Magic Wand to select the white background. Choose Select➛Inverse then choose Filter➛Alien Skin➛Cutout (X Offset: 2 pixels, Y Offset: 2 pixels, Blur: 4 pixel, Opacity: 60%, Shadow: Black, Fill: Transparent). Select the Move tool and use the arrow keys to offset Layer 1. Make Layer 1 copy visible.

TIP When you use a graphic more than once in a Web page, the graphic is still downloaded only once. Rules can be used multiple times throughout a Web page without affecting the download time.

VARIATIONS

Here we created a colored rectangle as the primary rule and then used the Type Mask tool to add the Zapf iron cross dingbats (Shift-2) with four spaces between each. After adding the dingbats choose white as the background color and press Delete.

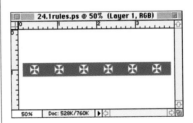

Rules can also be navigational elements. We used the Type Mask tool to create a line of circles (L in Zapf Dingbats) and used the Gradient tool to apply a gradient (foreground to background). We then added a single arrow (Option-Shift-; in Zapf Dingbats) at the end as a pointer.

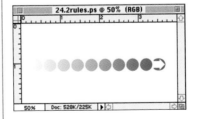

113

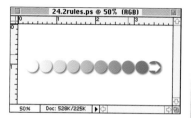

To finish the rule we added a drop shadow using Alien Skin drop shadow filter (X offset: 4, Y offset: 4 Blur: 8 Opacity: 65). ■

PART V

Buttons and Bullets

Buttons and bullets are place markers that help readers navigate through a Web site. The 'look' and 'feel' of a Web page is often dominated by buttons and bullets. While they are certainly not necessary on every Web page, buttons and bullets are important for helping visitors understand where they are, where they were, and where they could go next.

When used correctly buttons and bullets facilitate finding information quickly. But remember, too many buttons or bullets on a page can be as confusing as understanding the front panel of a VCR. Finding the right balance is key to supporting a successful interactive experience for Web site visitors.

A button should identify itself as an object meant to be pressed. Adding drop shadows to create a simulated 3D effect encourages visitors to interact with the button. Other techniques, such as an animated GIF (see pages 205 through 238), can be used to highlight special events, promotions, and other key information.

Basic Gradients

Gradients can be used to create a variety of effects for your buttons. This example gives your button a metallic or chrome effect.

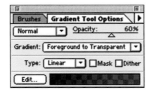

1 Create a new file. Double-click the Gradient tool and set the options to Mode: Normal, Opacity: 60%, Gradient: Foreground to Transparent (foreground is set to black), Type: Linear, Mask: on, and Dither: off (keeping dithering off helps keep the file size smaller when converted to GIF format).

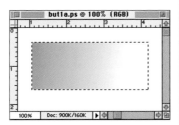

2 Make a selection for the button (the selection can be larger than the final button size—you can always shrink it later) and save the selection (Channel #4). With the Gradient tool, start outside the selection and click and drag across approximately 80% of the selection. Dragging on a diagonal angle will tilt the gradient for more visual interest.

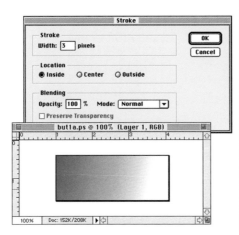

3 Choose Edit➔Stroke (Width: 3 pixels, Location: Inside, Mode: Normal). This creates a border around the button. The width can be any size, but be sure to set the Location radio button to Inside. This keeps the border inside the selection you saved as Channel #4.

VARIATIONS

Rainbow Gradient

This alternative to a plain border adds a sense of dimension to the button.

1 After Step 2, choose Select➞ Modify➞Border (Width: 6 pixels). Make the border twice as thick as you want the final version to be. Edit➞Fill (Foreground Color).

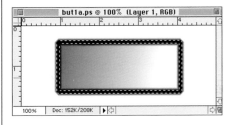

2 Load the selection Channel #4, Select➞Inverse, and press Delete. This fills the area around the button with the background color and gives the button sharp edges. Notice how the corners of the button have a mitered effect.

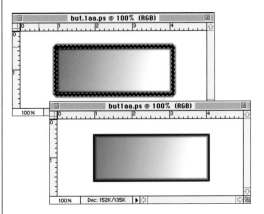

3 For this button, we set the Gradient tool to Spectrum (Opacity: 50%).

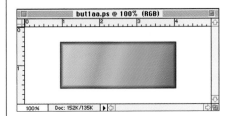

Metallic Gradient

Gradients on the vertical axis can be used to create metallic effects when they begin darker at the top and bottom and lighten towards the center. For this effect your foreground color should be black and your background color should be white.

1 Set the Gradient tool to Mode: Normal; Opacity: 65%; Gradient: Foreground to Transparent; Type: Linear; Mask: off; and Dither: off. Click the Edit button to access the Gradient Editor.

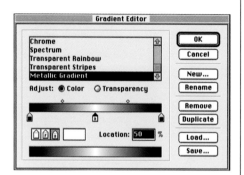

Click New to create a custom gradient. To add a new color click below the midpoint of the gradient bar. A new color icon appears where you clicked. Click the color icon with the B in it to change the color. The new color is your background color (in this case, white).

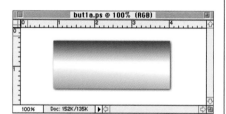

2 Choose Filter➔Distort➔Displace and use the default settings. A dialog box appears requesting that you choose a displacement map.

The Displacement Map function uses patterns that can be applied as dmaps (displacement maps). The maps are located inside the Photoshop Plug-ins folder. For this effect we chose Schnable Effect, a swirly line pattern. Locate the file Schnable Effect and click Open.

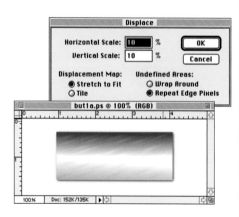

Crossing Gradients

Choose colors for the foreground and background and Load the selection Channel #4. Set the Gradient tool for Foreground to Background and drag the Gradient tool horizontally across the button. Choose Select➡Modify➡ Contract (16 pixels). (The frame size of the button is determined by the number of pixels you contract the selection.) Drag the Gradient tool across this selection in the opposite direction to create the second gradient.

In addition to being able to create your own gradients with multiple colors and blendings, each gradient contains a transparency mask to control the opacity of the gradient fill at different locations on the gradient bar. Click the Transparency radio button on the Gradient Editor to replace the transparency adjustment squares with the color adjustment squares. ■

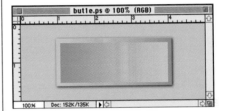

Radial Gradients

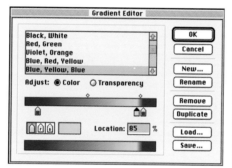

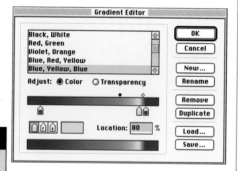

With Photoshop 4.0's new Gradient tool, simple and complex radial gradients can be applied to create an infinite range of stylized, decorative, and dimensional buttons.

1 Create a new file. Choose View➔Show Grid. With the Elliptical Marquee tool, make a round selection for your button.

2 Double-click the Gradient tool icon. (Opacity: 70%; Gradient: Blue, Yellow, Blue; Type: Radial; Dither: off). Click Edit. Select the yellow color square and type 85 in the Location entry box. Select the left-most diamond above the gradient bar and type 80 in the Location entry box.

TIP Gradients can be gradual or sharply defined. A sharply defined gradient can create an edge effect within your button while the gradual use of gradients creates a sense of depth. Adjusting the diamonds above the gradient bar will control the transition of the gradient.

120

TOOLBOX

Alien Skin's
Drop Shadow

3 Use the grid to locate the center of the selection and drag the Gradient tool from the center to the edge of your selection. Choose View➡Hide Grid.

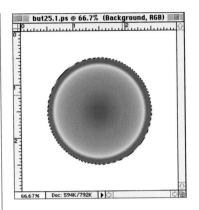

4 Choose Filter➡Render➡Lens Flare. (Brightness: 150%, Type: 105mm prime). The lens flare creates a highlight on the button.

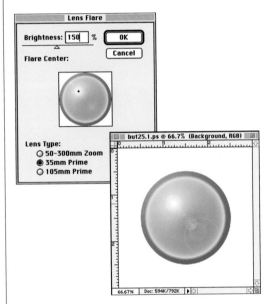

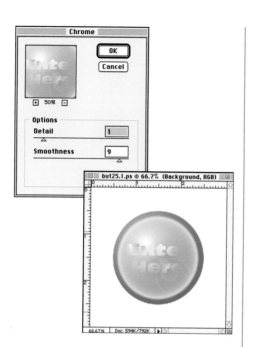

5 With the Type Mask tool, enter your text. Choose Filter➥ Sketch➥Chrome (Detail: 1, Smoothness: 9). Keep detail low so the filter doesn't interfere with the legibility of type. Save the selection (Channel #4).

6 To finish the button, we applied a drop shadow with the Alien Skin Drop Shadow filter and then brightened the text to improve readability. You can also apply a soft shadow (see page 72).

VARIATIONS

Linear Gradient

This button has a linear gradient instead of radial. We also changed the bright yellow to an orange.

Spectrum Gradient

For this variation we chose
Spectrum instead of Blue, Yellow,
Blue from the Gradient Tool dialog
box in Step 1. We also adjusted
the opacity of the gradient to
50%.

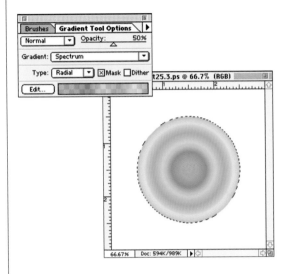

After we applied the gradient we
chose Filter➞Brush Strokes➞
Spatter (Spray Radius: 18,
Smoothness: 11) to break up the
gradient for a more organic feel.

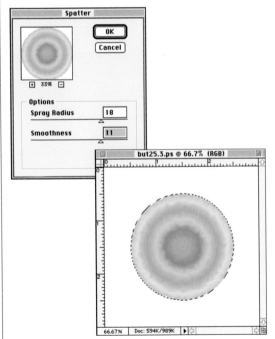

123

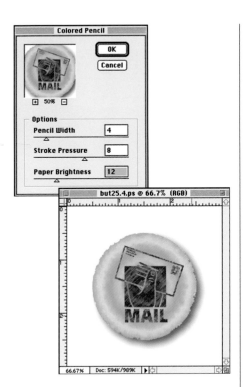

Finally, we added an icon and applied Filter➡Artistic➡ Colored Pencil (Pencil Width: 4, Stroke Pressure: 8, Paper Brightness: 12). ■

Bevel

Bevels have long been used as architecture and wood working details. They accent otherwise plain edges and add a finishing touch. On a Web page they can add dimension and depth to buttons. Photoshop's Lighting Effects filter is the primary tool for creating customized bevels.

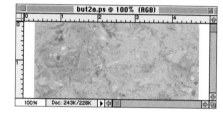

1 Open a file with a texture for your button. (There is a texture folder on the CD with a variety of textures.) Make a selection for your button and save the selection (Channel #4).

2 Choose Select➔Inverse and press Delete to fill the area surrounding the button with the background color.

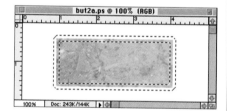

3 Select➔Inverse again to reselect the button. Choose Select➔Modify➔Border (8 pixels). This defines the width of the bevel. Save the selection as a new channel (Channel #5).

 To make the bevel even more defined, load the selection **Channel #5 and** make it the active channel. **Fill** the selection **with white. Select➔All and apply Filter➔Blur➔Gaussian Blur (3 pixels). Increasing the number of pixels for the blur increases the softness of the bevel even more.**

TOOLBOX

Alien Skin's
Inner Bevel
Outer Bevel

SuckingFish
DekoBoko
Frame Curtain

4 Load Channel #4 and choose Filter➞Render➞Lighting Effects. Use 2 o'clock Spotlight from the from the style presets. Choose Texture Channel: #5, and set the Height slider to 50%. To position the light on your object move the small circle in the center, to move the light futher or closer from the object expand or contract the outer circle.

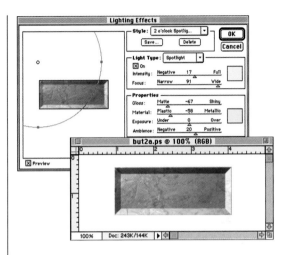

VARIATION

Alien Skin Filters

The Alien Skin commercial filter package contains two filters that make creating bevels a snap. The Inner Bevel filter applies the bevel inside of the selected area. Sliders give you control of bevel width, shadows, highlights, and light direction. The filter also contains a half-dozen preset bevels to choose from.

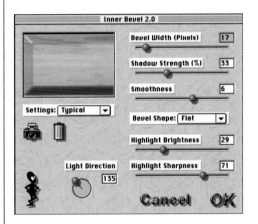

The filter even adds subtle detail to the bevel—note the highlight on the top-left corner.

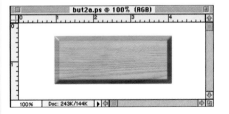

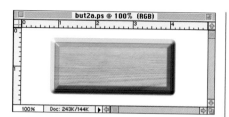

The Outer Bevel filter applies a bevel to the area outside of the selection. This is a great feature for making buttons look as if they are encased in the background.

SuckingFish Filters

A mailware (the author Naoto Arakawa in Japan simply requests an email if you like his filters) filter package with a bevel filter is the SuckingFish Series of filters. Not quite as feature-rich as the Alien Skin bevel filters, the DekoBoko filter creates one-step bevels and includes an inverse option that can be used to create depressed buttons.

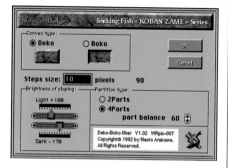

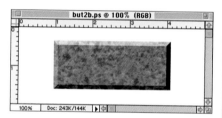

The SuckingFish filters are for the Macintosh only and are on the Photoshop Web Magic CD-ROM.

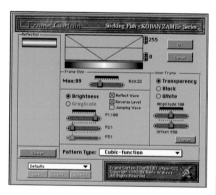

Included in the SuckingFish Series is the Frame Curtain filter, which converts waveforms into grayscale frames for objects. It comes with over 30 preset frames and offers options for creating an unlimited number of variations. ■

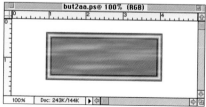

Multicolored Variations

Color-coding Web sites can assist visitors in finding their way around the site or help identify where they are. The Photoshop Variations filter can be used to create an entire site's worth of color-coded buttons at once.

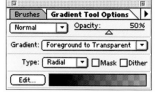

1 Create a new file, then make a selection for the button and save the selection as a new channel (Channel #4). Double-click the Gradient tool icon to access the Gradient Options palette (Mode: Normal, Opacity: 50%, Gradient: Foreground to Transparent, Type: Radial, Mask: on, Dither: off).

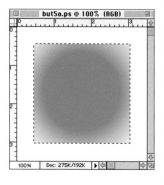

2 Click OK and drag to create a gradient, beginning in the center of the image and ending slightly outside one of the selection's corners.

130

TOOLBOX

Alien Skin's Inner Bevel

3 Apply a bevel using Alien Skin Inner Bevel. If you don't have the Alien Skin filter, follow the steps in the Bevel Button section (pages 126-129) to create the bevel or skip this step.

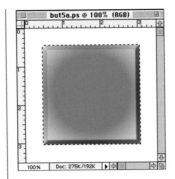

4 To create a consistent look across the site we used a globe from the Carta font at 150 points. With the Type Mask tool, enter your dingbat text.

5 With the selection active on the background, choose Image➧ Adjust➧Brightness/Contrast (Brightness: +70). If you prefer to use an icon from another source, pasting the icon into the file will automatically create a new layer. You can then adjust the brightness/contrast of the layer by adding an adjustment layer Layer➧New➧Adjustment Layer: Brightness/Contrast.

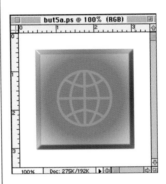

6 Load the selection Channel #4 and choose Image➧Adjust➧ Variations. You have six color-coded buttons surrounding your original gray button in the center.

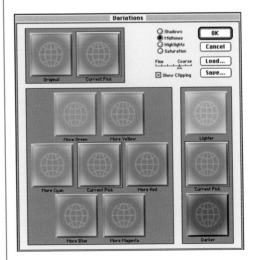

131

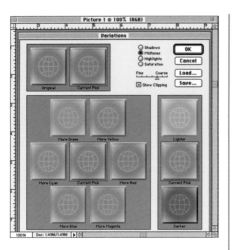

7 To use this image you will have to take a screen-snapshot of it. On a Mac (Command-Shift-3) you will hear what sounds like a camera click. The file is saved as a PICT file named Picture 1 on your start-up disk. On Windows use F13 (Print Screen on some keyboards). The file is sent to the Clipboard and can be pasted into a new file.

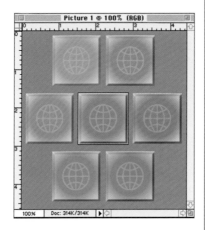

8 On a Mac Open Picture 1. [On Windows create a new file and paste the clipboard into the file.] Crop the image to select the box containing the colored buttons. Select the Eyedropper tool. Hold down the option key while picking up the background gray from the image to assign it as your background color. Remove the type labels by marqueeing around the type and pressing delete.

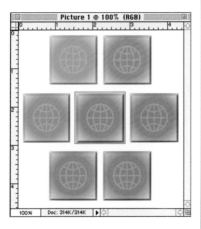

9 Choose a new background color (we used white). Use the Magic Wand tool (Tolerance: 2) to select the gray background and press Delete to fill the background with your selected color.

10 Choose Select➡Inverse. Save the selection (Channel #4). This channel can be used to apply a drop shadow or glow effect to the buttons. You can save the entire image as a GIF to be used as an imagemap on your Web pages. Or crop, copy, and paste each button to a new file for use as separate buttons.

VARIATION

This variation creates rectangular buttons and easy to do, one step edge effects.

1 Create a new file, make a selection for the button, and save the selection (Channel #4). To create a basic background texture choose Filter➡Sketch➡Note Paper (Image Balance: 25, Graininess: 12, Relief: 11.)

2 Choose Image➡Adjust➡ Variations and follow Steps 6 through 9.

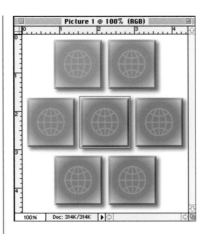

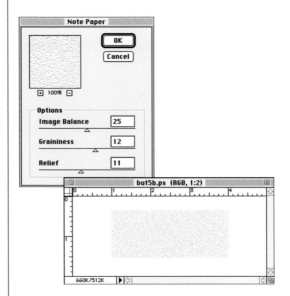

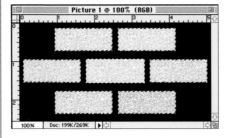

133

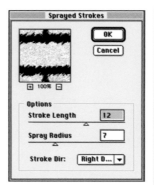

3 With the buttons selected choose Select➔Modify➔Contract (8 pixels), then choose Select➔ Inverse. Choose Filter➔Brush Strokes➔Sprayed Strokes (Stroke Length: 12, Spray Radius: 7, Stroke Direction: Right Diagonal).

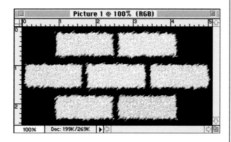

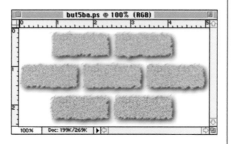

4 You can now use the Eyedropper tool to select the background as in Step 9. ■

Globe Buttons

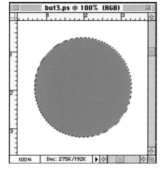

The three-dimensional aspect of spheres and globes is created by the way light hits an object and creates highlights and shadows. Photoshop's Lighting Effects filter helps to bring these aspects of 3D to flat illustration.

1 Create a new file (Contents: White). Make a round selection and save the selection as a new channel (Channel #4). Select a color of your choice for the background color. Press Delete to fill your selection with color. Leave the sphere selected.

TIP Work with the background color you intend to use for your final Web page. By keeping the colors consistent the anti-aliased pixels around the edges of your object will blend cleanly with your background.

2 To create a sphere with soft reflective qualities choose Filter➤Render➤Lighting Effects. Match the settings shown in the figure. You'll need to expand the light's area and change the light's center. Once you are pleased with the effect save the settings as a new Style named Soft Sphere for future use.

To tweak the light, adjust the size of the circle in the Preview box and vary the Intensity and Focus settings. Once you are pleased with the settings, save them. Click OK and you have a sphere.

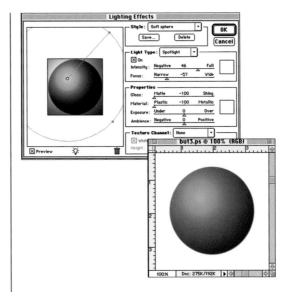

VARIATIONS

Metallic Reflection

To create a sphere with more reflective highlights use the settings shown in the figure. By increasing the Gloss settings the highlight in the center of the light will be brighter, increasing the overall brightness of the image.

TIP Light has a gray tint when it reflects off metal objects; light reflecting off of plastic retains more of the original hue of the object.

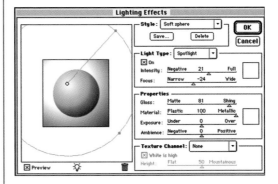

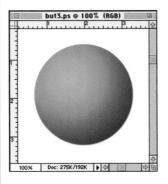

137

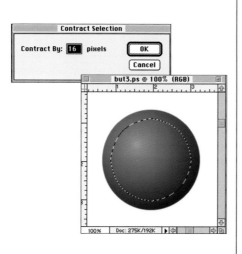

Indented Sphere

In this example we created an indent in the center of the button to add a feeling of depth.

1 After creating the initial sphere choose Select➡Modify➡Contract (16 pixels).

Contract Selection

Contract By: 16 pixels   OK   Cancel

but3.ps @ 100% (RGB)
100%   Doc: 275K/192K

2 Choose Layer➡Transform➡ Rotate (90°CW). The globe appears to be inverted and receding into the button.

but3.ps @ 100% (RGB)
100%   Doc: 275K/192K

Feathered Indent

For this button we feathered the selection by 4 pixels (Select➡ Feather) before rotating the center section.

Feather Selection

Feather Radius: 4 pixels   OK   Cancel

but3.ps @ 100% (RGB)
100%   Doc: 275K/192K

Beveled Globe

1 After creating the initial sphere, choose Select➤Modify➤Contract (16 pixels), then save as a new selection (Channel #5). Next, Select➤Load Selection (Channel #4, New Selection); and Select➤Load Selection (Channel #5, Subtract from Selection). Save as a new channel (Channel #6).

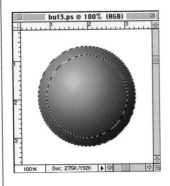

2 Load the selection Channel #4. Make Channel #6 visible. Choose Filter➤Blur➤Gaussian Blur (3 pixels) to soften the edge of the bevel.

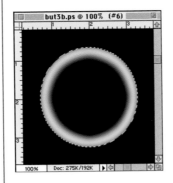

3 With Channel #4 still selected, return to the composite channel, and choose Filter➤Render➤ Lighting Effects. In the Lighting Effects dialog box, set the Texture Channel to Channel #6 and rotate the light source to be opposite the globe's original light source.

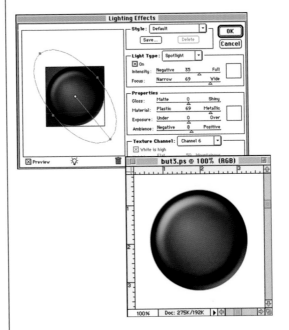

139

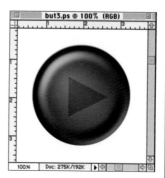

4 To finish the button we added a triangle-shaped dingbat as a directional arrow. The dingbat was selected and saved as Channel #7. The layer was then hidden and the background made active. With the selection on the background layer, choose Image➔ Adjust➔Brightness/Contrast (Brightness: -20%). ∎

Spherized Photos

Photographs can be given a convincing 3D effect, appearing to wrap around a globe, by using both the Spherize and Lighting Effects filters. In this example we used a photograph from VisualSoftware's Textures for Professionals CD-ROM.

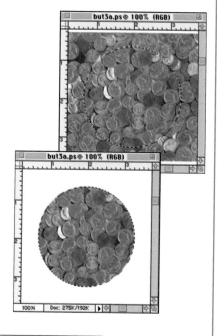

1 Open a file containing a photograph of your choice. Make a round selection and save the selection as a new channel (Channel #4). Select a background color of your choice. Choose Select➔ Inverse then press delete to fill with the background color.

TOOLBOX

Alien Skin's Outer Bevel

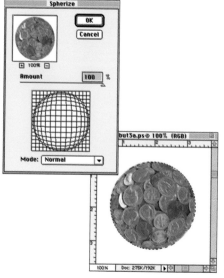

2 Invert the selection again (or load selection Channel #4) and choose Filter➔Distort➔Spherize (Amount: 100%, Mode: normal). If parts of your image distort too heavily, try lower settings.

3 Choose Filter➔Render➔Lighting Effects. Select 2 o'clock Spotlight from the Style menu. You may need to experiment to find settings that work best with your photograph.

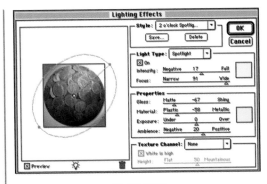

TIP For the most realistic 3D effect, match the direction of the light with the direction of the primary light source in the photograph.

4 Use the Type Mask tool to enter the text. Save text as a new channel (Channel #5) and then hide the new layer. Make Channel #5 active (Command-5) [Control-5]. Select➔All and choose Filter➔Distort➔Spherize (100%, Normal).

143

5 Return to the Composite channel (Command-~ [Control-~]. Load the Channel #5 selection to make the type selection active. Choose Image➞Adjust➞Brightness/Contrast (Brightness: +50, Contrast: -10).

6 The final step is to apply a drop shadow. We used the Alien Skin Drop Shadow filter (x and y offset 3 pixels, Blur 5 pixels, and Opacity 50%). Export to GIF format and make the background color transparent when saving as a GIF.

VARIATION

To make the curved button appear as if it is recessed into a console with a frame we used the Alien Skin Outer Bevel filter with Settings: Button. ■

Gray on Gray

The default background color for Netscape Navigator, Internet Explorer, and most other browsers is gray. Because it is so neutral, gray works well in Web sites where utility and function are the primary focus. Many of Photoshop's filters can be used to create textures to make attractive buttons in the gray range.

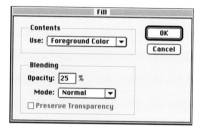

1 Create a new file. Choose Edit➔Fill (Use Black, Opacity: 25%). This will create a 25% gray screen—the same as browser default gray (the hexadecimal value of default gray on a Web page is C3C3C3—place this value in the Body command to keep a gray page gray even if a user has defined a different default background color).

2 Create a rectangular selection for the button and save the selection (Channel #4). Choose Filter➔Sketch➔Halftone Pattern (Size: 1, Screen Type: Line, Contrast: 0). You can create larger lines by increasing the Size setting.

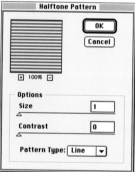

TOOLBOX

Alien Skin's
Drop Shadow
Inner Bevel
Patchwork

KPT Page Curl

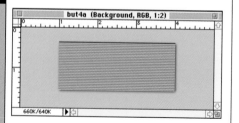

3 Create a drop shadow using Alien Skin Drop Shadow filter (x, y offset: 3 pixels, blur: 6 pixels, and opacity: 70%) or follow the Soft Shadow exercise on page 72.

4 Select all and choose Filter➡️ Distort➡️Wave. The Wave filter is capable of a multitude of effects and distortions. For this effect we chose Number of Generators: 1; Type: Sine Wavelength: Min: 10; Max: 166, Amplitude: Min: 5; Max: 35. Undefined Areas: Repeat edge pixels. The settings you use can vary as you explore the various Wave functions. Keep Number of Generators set to one while adjusting the Wavelength and Amplitude sliders for a wide range of effects and distortions. Click the Randomize button for different wave effects.

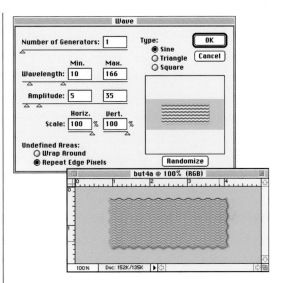

 Any of the buttons in this exercise, or in this book, can be colorized by using the Hue/Saturation function from the Image menu. Check the Colorize box on the Hue/Saturation dialog box. Your image will turn a bright red. Lower the saturation to around 50% and then select a new color for your button with the Hue slider.

VARIATIONS

Photoshop 4.0's extended selection of filters makes it easy to create an almost limitless number patterns and textures for buttons.

147

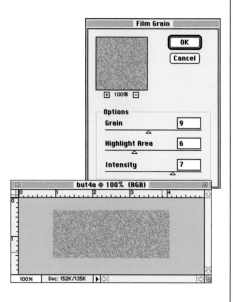

Crosshatch Button

1 Follow Step 1 to create a 25% gray background and make a selection for your button. Choose Filter➔Artistic➔Film Grain (Grain: 9, Highlight Area: 6, Highlight Intensity: 7). To try variations on the slider settings click Preview and press apply when you have a texture you like.

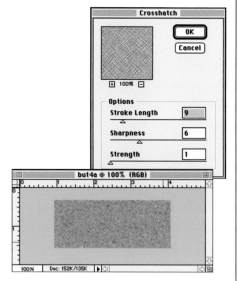

2 Choose Filter➔Brush Strokes➔ Crosshatch (Stroke Length: 9, Sharpness: 6, Strength: 1). Keeping the Sharpness and Strength settings low produces a diffused effect that won't interfere with the legibility of the type on the button.

3 For the type treatment on this button we stuck with gray tones using a 25% gray (same as the background color) for the first word and 75% gray for the second word, "Here."

Background Bevels

Beveled buttons that are the same color as the background have a very neat look and create the appearance of being fully integrated into the Web page.

1 Follow Step 1 to create a 25% gray background and make a selection for your button. We then applied the Alien Skin Inner Bevel filter (Low Flat). If you do not have this filter, you can create a bevel by following Steps 3 and 4 in the Beveled Button exercise (page 126).

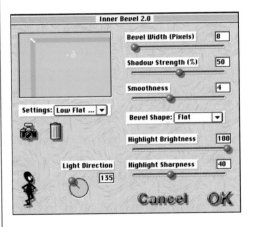

2 Make a rectangular selection containing about 80% of the area inside the button. Choose Image➔ Adjust➔Brightness/Contrast (Brightness: +25, Contrast: 0).

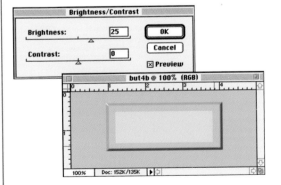

Velcro

This combination of Photoshop 4.0 filters can make buttons look like fabric labels or even strips of velcro.

1 Follow Step 1 to create a 25% gray background and make a selection for your button. Choose Filter➔Texture➔Patchwork (Square Size: 4, Relief: 8).

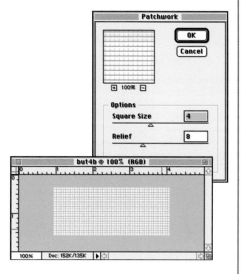

2 With the button still selected, choose Filter➔Artistic➔Colored Pencil (Pencil Width: 4; Stroke Pressure: 8, Paper Brightness: 25). Notice how this filter creates what appears to be a border around the button. Export to GIF format.

3 We used MetaTools KPT Page Curl filter and finished the button by adding a drop shadow.

This filter enables you to adjust the direction and degree of curl by clicking and dragging. When used sparingly on Web pages, the Curl filter adds an interesting 3-D focal point for important buttons or information. ■

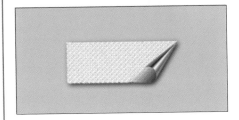

Pill Shaped

Pill-shaped buttons—not quite rectangles and not quite ovals—can be used to add a distinctive look to Web pages.

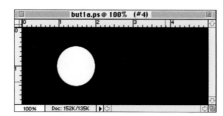

1 Create a new file. Double-click the Marquee icon and select the elliptical Marquee tool. Hold down the Shift key while using the Marquee tool to make a round selection for the button. Save the selection (Channel #4). Make Channel #4 visible.

2 Select the rectangular Marquee tool. Carefully draw a rectangular selection cutting through the center, even with the top and bottom of the circle, and extending about 1/2 of the width of your intended button. You might want to zoom in to make the image as large as possible.

3 Choose Edit➤Fill (Use: White, Opacity: 100%, Mode: Normal). Load the selection Channel #4.

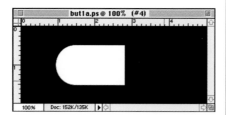

4 Copy and paste your selection to create a floating selection. Choose Layer➤Transform➤Flip➤ Horizontal. Place the flipped selection to complete the other side of the pill. Adjust the width of the pill by overlapping the selection, if you want.

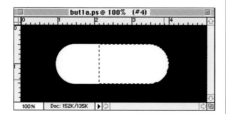

152

5 Duplicate Channel #4 (Channel #5). Set the Marquee tool to elliptical. Make Channel #5 active and make a long elliptical selection across the bottom half of the button. Next we'll add some highlight to the selection.

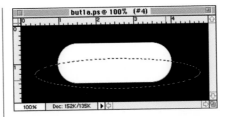

6 Choose Edit➤Fill (Use: Black, Opacity: 100%, Mode: Normal) Deselect. Soften the edges with Filter➤Blur➤Gaussian Blur (6 pixels). More blur will create a softer highlight, less blur a sharper, more defined highlight.

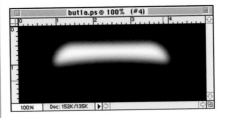

7 Return to the composite channel. Load the selection Channel #4, and fill the selection with a color of your choice. We used the RGB values 94, 208, 255 in this example. Then, with Channel #4 still selected, load the selection Channel #5 (Subtract from Selection).

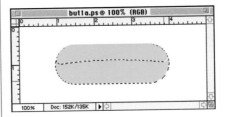

8 Choose Image➤Adjust➤ Brightness/Contast (Brightness: –50, Contrast: 0). The top half of the button should appear lighter, as if it is a curved cylinder with a light source shining from above.

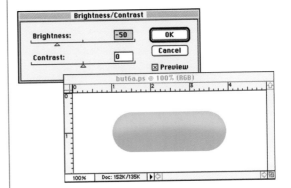

153

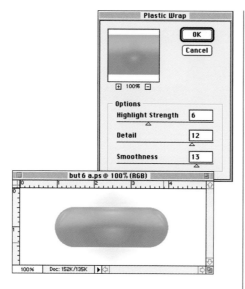

9 To add some subtle highlights to the button use Filters➛Artistic➛ Plastic Wrap (Highlight Strength: 6, Detail: 12, Smoothness: 13). This filter produces different effects depending upon the size of the selection and color and variations in the image. Try the above settings as a starting point and experiment from there.

10 To increase the illusion of light hitting the button from above, with the button still selected, choose Filter➛Render➛Lighting Effects. Choose the preset Style: Parallel Directional. This style setting defaults to a blue light tint (like placing a colored gel over a light). Adjust the tint to a hue similar but darker than the color of your button.

TIP After you become comfortable using the Lighting Effects filter, try different combinations of color for Light Type and Properties. You will find that "painting with light" will add considerable realism and subtlety to your art.

11 To finish the button we used a funky typeface named Dogs on Mars. To enhance the carved look of the lettering we used the Alien Skin Carve filter with a Bevel Width set to 3 pixels. Finally, export as a GIF.

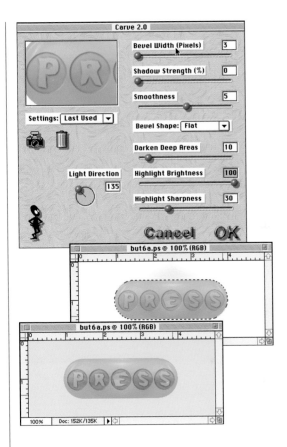

VARIATION

To create this silver bullet we used the lighting effects texture channel with high metallic properties.

Following Step 6 we returned to the composite channel, loaded the selection, and (Channel #4) chose Edit→Stroke (Width: 3 pixels, Location: Inside, Opacity: 100%, Mode: Normal) to create a solid black border around the button.

155

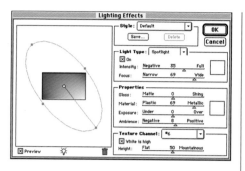

We chose Filter➥Render➥Lighting Effects (Style: Default) and assigned Channel #5 as the Texture Channel. The results were a bit too contrasting and harsh. We used the undo key and tried it again. To compensate, we made a second copy of Channel #5 (Channel #6) and applied an additional Gaussian Blur of 6 pixels to the channel. We then tried the Lighting Effects filter again using Channel #6 for this result. ■

Glass

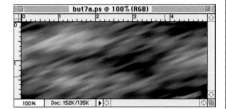

In the past, creating glass effects required a fairly complicated series of processes including creating multiple channels, calculation adjustments, and smudging to replicate the unique reflective and refractive qualities of glass. In Photoshop 4.0 that process has been made much easier with the introduction of the Glass filter.

1 Open a file containing a texture of your choice (Sample textures can be found on the CD in the Web Magic folder) or create a new file and create a texture. For this example we used MetaTools KPT Texture Explorer and chose a preset texture. Make a selection for your button and save the selection (Channel #4). For this exercise we used the pill shape mask (from Technique #32), but you can use any shape you choose.

2 Choose Image➥Adjust➥ Brightness/Contrast (Brightness: +65, Contrast: -10). Increasing the brightness and lowering the contrast adds a subtle gray glass-like haze to the image.

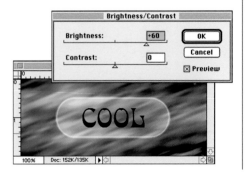

3 Choose Select➥Modify➥Border (3 pixels), then choose Image➥ Adjust➥Brightness/Contrast (Brightness: +60, Contrast: 0). This creates the light glow around the object. Use the Type Mask tool to enter the type. Save the type selection (Channel #5).

158

4 Choose Image➔Adjust➔ Brightness/Contrast (Brightness: +60, Contrast: 0). This makes the text appear transparent and gives it the same degree of brightness as the button's border. As an optional step we applied a drop shadow using Alien Skin 2.0 with an x and y offset of 3 pixels, a 12 pixel blur, and opacity of 40%. Or, refer to page 70, "Shadows for Buttons."

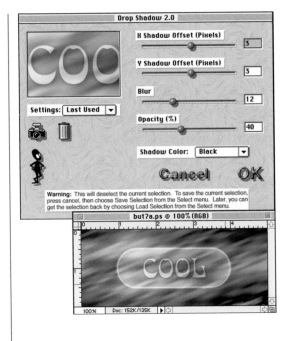

5 Load the selection Channel #4, then load the selection Channel #5 (Subtract from Selection).

6 Choose Filter➔Glass (Frosted, Scaling: 30% 100%). Adjust the Effect Controls to your liking. We used Distortion at 5 and Smoothness at 3. Use the Preview button to fine tune your settings and apply. Finally, export as a GIF.

159

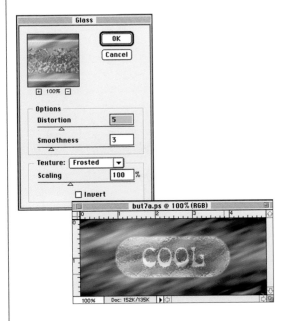

The Glass Surface Controls dialog box contains 4 different textures: frosted, blocks, canvas, and tiny lens, but you can also import a custom PICT file as a texture. Try using them in combination for glass on glass effects. (Frosted glass buttons on a stained glass title plaque, for example.)

VARIATION

For this variation on glass buttons we created a glass border with a stained glass insert in the center.

First we chose a different texture from MetaTools KPT Texture Explorer and filled our button selection with it. Save the selection (Channel #4). We choose Selection➛Modify➛Contract (16 pixels) and saved the result as a new channel (Channel #5).

Loading the selection Channel #4, then loading the selection Channel #5 (Subtract from Selection) created the border selection that was saved as a new channel (Channel #6).

With Channel #6 selected we applied the Glass filter with tiny lens chosen as the texture.

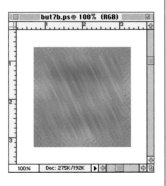

A glow was applied around the center box as described in Step 3.

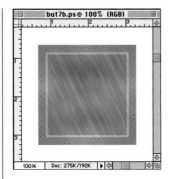

With Channel #5 selected, we chose Filter➡Stained Glass (Cell Size: 10, Border Thickness: 4, Light Intensity: 3). You can almost feel the light shining through the window. ■

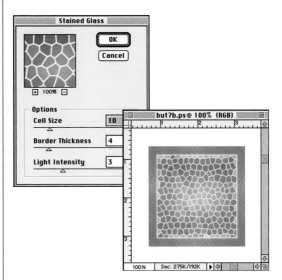

Concentric Circles

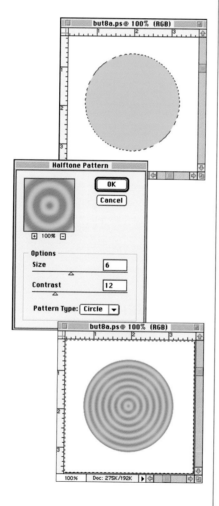

Besides creating halftone dots, Photoshop 4.0's new Halftone Screen filter can create concentric circles—when someone clicks a bulls-eye button they know they are going someplace important.

1 Create a new file. Double-click the Marquee tool and select Elliptical from the Shape pop-up menu that appears. With the Marquee tool selected, hold down the Shift key to make a circular selection.

2 Choose the foreground and background colors. In this case we chose yellow (RGB: 200, 213, 34) for the foreground and aqua (RGB: 89, 150, 157) for the background. Choose Filter➔Halftone Pattern (Size: 6, Contrast: 12, Screen Type: Circle). The Size slider adjusts the width of the circles.

3 Select➡All and choose
Filter➡Distort➡Spherize (Amount:
100%, Mode: Horizontal). This
will stretch the button along the
horizontal axis to create a shape
that is not quite an ellipse but
more like a rounded rectangle.

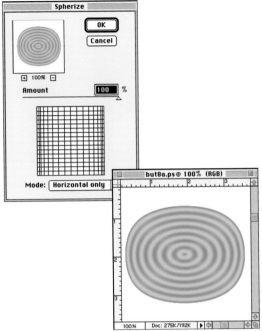

4 To select the new button shape,
double-click the Magic Wand icon
and set the options (Tolerance to
2, Anti-aliased: on). Click the
white area surrounding the button. Choose Select➡Inverse, and
save the selection as a new channel (Channel #4).

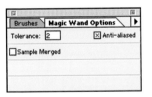

163

5 Choose Filter➡Reticulation
(Density: 20, Black Level: 31,
White Level: 20). This adds some
texture to mimic the rough surface
of a cork dart board.

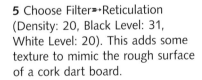

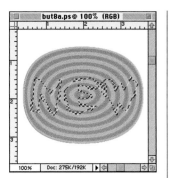

6 To add transparent type to the button, choose the Type Mask tool, enter the text and save the type selection as a new channel (Channel #5).

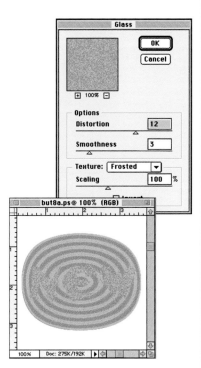

7 With the type outline selected on the background layer, choose Filter➭Glass (Distortion: 12, Smoothness: 3, Texture: Frosted, Scaling 100%).

8 To define the type from the background choose Image➥ Adjust➥Hue/Saturation. We used a Hue setting of -160, Saturation 0, and Lightness -35. You may want to adjust these settings to find the ones that work best with your color scheme.

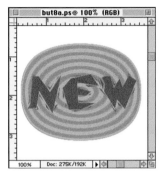

9 To make a rectangular button, use the rectangular Marquee tool to make a selection, and choose Select➥Inverse. Switch to the default colors and press the Delete key to fill the selection with white. Select➥Inverse. Add a drop shadow. For the drop shadow we used the Alien Skin Drop Shadow 2.0 filter.

TIP Many of Photoshop 4.0's new filters enable you to save your settings. This makes it easier and faster to repeat your favorite looks.

165

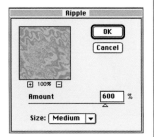

Swirled Ripples

To create this somewhat beat-up looking button, do steps 1 and 2, then choose Filters➥Distort➥ Ripple (Amount: 600, Size: Medium).

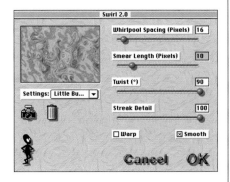

Instead of using the Glass filter in Step 6 we used Alien Skin's Swirl filter with Little Bubbles selected from the filter's preset pop-up menu.

Finally we chose the Alien Skin Glow filter to add a white glow around the type and added a drop shadow to the button.

Twirled Halftone

On this variation we set the halftone screen filter at its smallest setting (Size: 1, Screen Type: Circle, Contrast: 5).

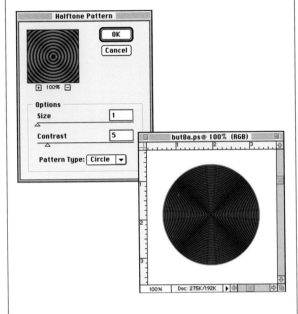

To generate a moiré pattern, we then reapplied the halftone pattern with the Screen Type set to dot (Size: 3, Contrast 5, Screen Type: Dot).

167

Depending on what colors you chose, the combination of the two filters might make the image appear very dark. To adjust for this we chose Image⇒Adjust⇒Brightness/Contrast (Brightness: +51, Contrast: +60)

Finally, to add a sense of motion to the button we applied Filter⇒Distort⇒Twirl (Angle: 225). ■

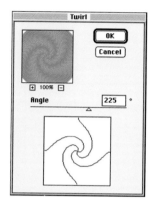

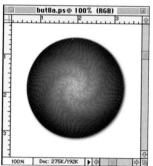

Directional Buttons

Buttons are intended to take you places; this button helps stress that point.

1 Create a new file. Create a square selection for your button (hold down the Shift key while creating the selection to keep it square) and save the selection (Channel #4). Choose foreground and background colors and press Delete to fill the selection with your background color. Select⇒ None.

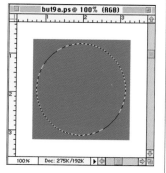

2 Double-click the Marquee tool and select Elliptical from the Shape pop-up menu in the options palette. Hold down the Shift key to make a circular selection inside the square selection as shown in the figure. Save the selection (Channel #5).

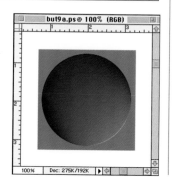

3 Load the selection Channel #4. Choose Filter⇒Render⇒Lighting effects (Texture Channel: Channel #5, White is high, Height: 50). Adjust the points on the circle in the lighting preview box to match the figure. To tweak the light, adjust the light's position and focus by moving the circles in the preview box. Save your changes to this panel.

4 With Channel #4 still selected, load the selection Channel #5 (Subtract from Selection). Save the new selection (Channel #6).

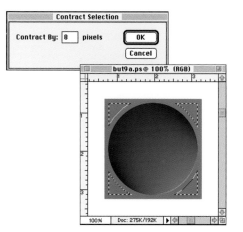

5 Choose Selection➞Modify➞ Contract Selection (Contract By: 8 pixels). Save the new selection, choosing Channel #6 instead of New to overwrite the existing Channel #6, which is not needed again.

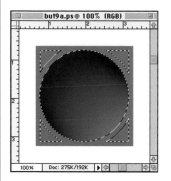

6 Load the selection Channel #5 (Add to Selection). Save as a new selection (Channel #7).

171

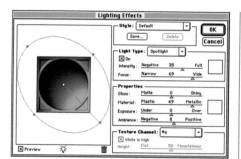

7 Load the selection Channel #4 and then choose Filter➔Render➔ Lighting Effects. Select Channel #7 as the Texture Channel. Adjust the points on the circle in the lighting preview box to match the figure.

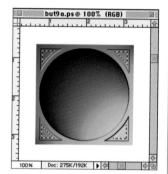

8 Load the selection Channel #6 and then choose Select➔Modify➔ Contract Selection (3 pixels).

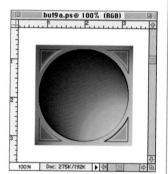

9 Choose Image➔Brightness/ Contrast (Brightness: -30, Contrast: 0). This creates a darker accent triangle in each corner.

10 To finish the button, we added transparent type. Enter the text using the Type Mask tool, and save the type selection as a new channel (Channel #8).

11 To brighten the text, Choose Image➔Adjust➔Brightness/Con- trast (Brightness: +50, Contrast: 0). We added a drop shadow using Alien Skin's Drop Shadow 2.0 filter with a 2 pixel X and Y Offset, a 4 pixel Blur, and Opacity set to 50%.

VARIATIONS

To make this button point to compass directions, follow the directions through Step 9, then switch to default colors. Load the selection Channel #4, and choose Layer➡Transform➡Numeric...➡ Rotate (Angle 45 degrees).

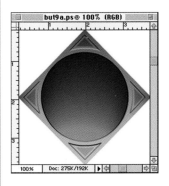

This multi-directional button was created by selecting a color for the background before rotating the selection 45 degrees.

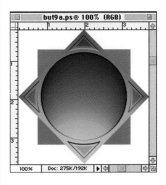

We applied a bevel effect here by loading Channel #5, contracting the selection by 8 pixels, and feathering it by 2 pixels. We then rotated the contracted selection 180 degrees (Layer➡Transform➡ Rotate 180°). ■

173

Objects on Buttons

Photoshop's path tool is used to turn photographic images into decorative buttons and icons. Image processing filters such as Ink Outline and Watercolor are used to create a wide range of illustrative effects.

1 Open the file containing the image you will be using for your button (the crafts stand photo can be found on the CD in the Web Magic folder).

2 Zoom in to fill your screen with the image detail that you are going to crop. Choose the Pen tool from the toolbox. Define the outline of the object, placing anchor points where needed.

TIP You can adjust the portion of the image you are viewing without deselecting the Path tool. When you move your cursor to the window's scroll-bars, the pointer returns.

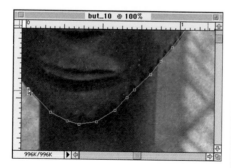

3 After you have finished outlining your selection, choose Make Selection from the Paths palette pop-up menu. Save the selection (Channel #4). Return to the Paths palette pop-up menu and Turn off Path (Paths palette pop-up menu).

4 Choose Selection➥Inverse. Press the Delete key to get rid of the photograph outside of your selection.

5 To create a background pattern for this object we chose Filter➥Render➥Clouds. A single pass of the Clouds filter is very subtle and light, so we applied the filter a second time.

6 Load channel selection #4. We used Alien Skin Glow filter with Settings: Diffuse to add a light white glow around the object. Then we added the Alien Skin Drop Shadow filter with an X and Y Offset of 8 pixels, Blur: 10 pixels, and Opacity: 90%.

7 Make a rectangular selection around the object to define the button (leave room to add the type), and save as a new selection (Channel #5).

8 Choose Select➥Modify➥Border (6 pixels) and then choose Image➥Adjust➥Brightness/Contrast (Brightness: +32, Contrast: 0).

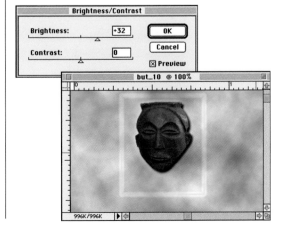

9 Add type to the button. Choose Select➡Load Selection (Channel #5), then crop the file: Image➡ Crop. Save as a JPEG.

VARIATIONS

Weathered Bronze

We were able change the texture of the African icon to a weathered bronze look by using the Ink Outlines filter. With the mask selected (Channel #4), choose Filter➡Brush Strokes➡Ink Outlines (Stroke Length: 4, Dark Intensity: 20, Light Intensity: 10).

This filter lowered the contrast and overall made the image much darker. To adjust for this, choose Image➡Adjust➡Brightness/ Contrast (Brightness: +26, Contrast: +70).

We created a copper-like effect on the mask with the Watercolor filter. With the mask selected (Channel #4), choose Filter➥ Artistic➥Watercolor (Brush Detail: 13, Shadow Intensity: 1, Texture: 1).

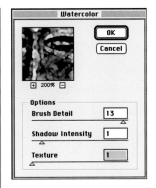

After applying this filter we adjusted brightness and contrast. Choose Image➥Adjust➥Brightness/ Contrast (Brightness: +20, Contrast: +72). ■

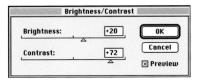

177

PART VI

Menu Bars

Menu bars are the keystone of a Web site's navigational system. They are the third level of user interface after the site visitors' computer operating systems and their browsers or interconnect systems.

The menu bar defines the architecture of your Web site's interface by displaying discrete, consistent information through all levels of interactivity. The menu prioritizes information and sets the main topics, headings, and locations within the site.

A typical menu bar for a site will contain links to areas such as:

- The home page

- The main index or table of contents page

- The about us or our product page

- Frequently Asked Questions (FAQs)

- Forums or chat rooms

- A contact page for getting in touch via email or for linking to sales and service support groups

In the following exercises, we demonstrate how to use Photoshop to build a variety of menu bar styles, including folder tabs. We recommend testing any menu bar—depending upon the overall organization and style of your Web page design, some menu bars styles will work better than others.

Tabs

This exercise uses HTML's 0 margin and borderless frames functionality that has been developed for 3.0 browsers. The final effect will have the appearance of multiple file folder tabs across the top of the Web page, but it will really be one image that we cut apart and import in segments.

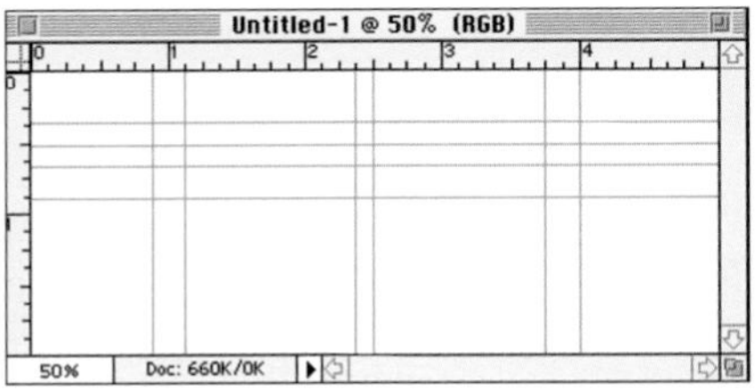

1 Create a new file and save it as a Photoshop document (38a.ps). The tabs are 1¼ inches wide, with ⅛ inch between them.

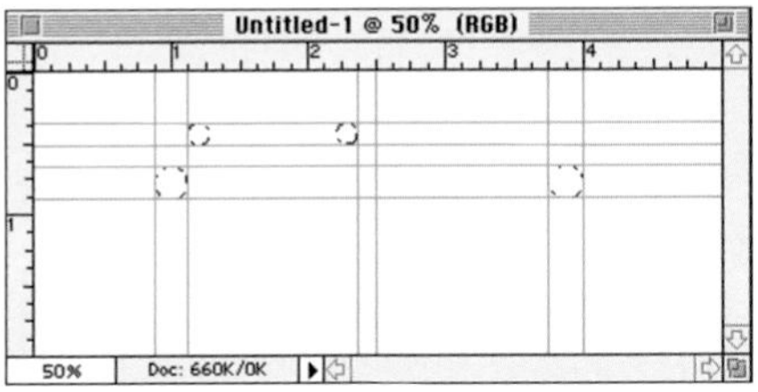

2 With the Elliptical Marquee tool, select circular areas inside the guidelines at the top of the tab and sides of the folders, as shown in the figure. Hold down the Shift key to add to the selection.

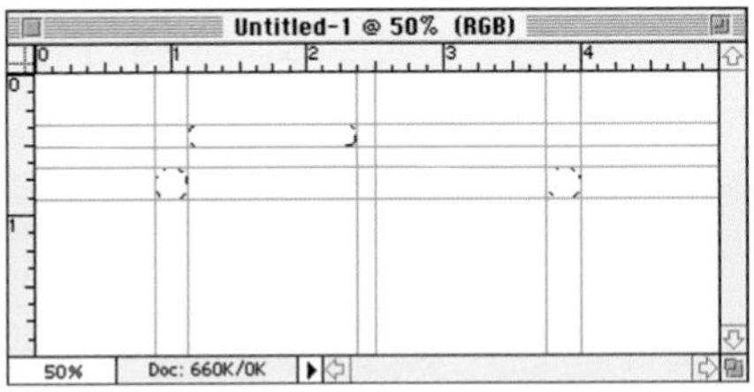

3 With the Rectangular Marquee tool, hold down the Shift key to add to the previous selection and select the space between the top two circles.

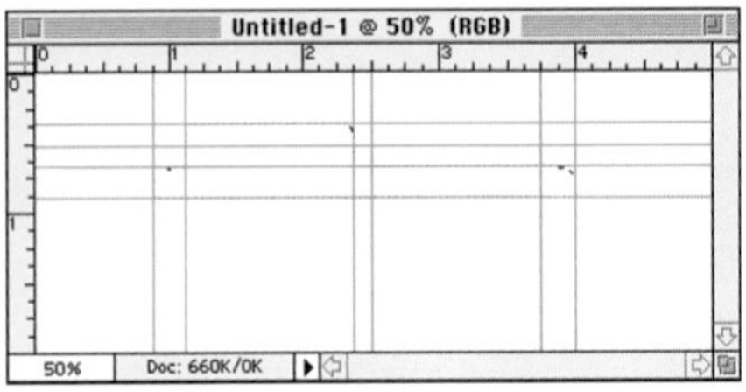

4 Continue to add to the selection, connecting all the circles incorporating them into one selection. For the bottom left and right corners, you will need to drag out the selection to the corners of the guidelines to make them square. Save the selection (Channel #4).

5 Click the New Channel icon in the Channels palette to make a new empty channel (Channel #5). With the Channels palette still active, load channel selection #4 into Channel #5. Choose Layer➛ Transform➛Flip Horizontal. Fill the selection with the foreground color (white).

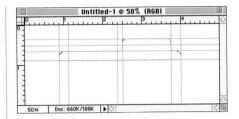

6 Return to the composite channel. Fill the background with a color. Create a new layer (drop-shadow 1) and load the left tab selection (Channel #4). Choose Select➛Feather (5 pixels).

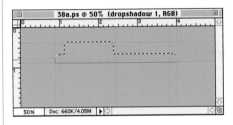

7 Fill the selection with black.

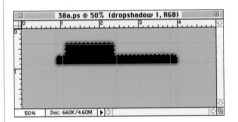

8 Create a new layer (back tab) and load the left tab selection. Fill it with 50% black.

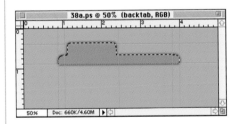

9 Create a new layer (Type Layer 1). Enter the text.

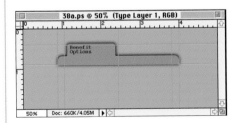

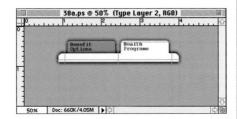

10 Repeat Steps 6 through 9 naming the layers dropshadow 2, front tab, and type layer 2. Feather and fill the drop shadow layer as in Steps 5 and 6 with black. Fill the Front Tab layer selection with white and enter the type on Type Layer 2.

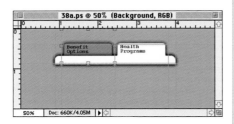

11 Move the bottom guideline up slightly by clicking it and dragging, enough to cut off the bottom drop shadow when you crop it. Save the image.

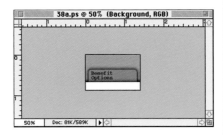

12 With the Crop tool, drag your pointer across the image within the guidelines that define the left tab.

13 Double-click the image to crop it. Export to GIF format.

14 Revert to the original image (38a.ps). With the Crop tool, select the area defining the right tab. Double-click to crop it. Export to GIF format.

15 Revert to the original image (38a.ps). With the Crop tool, select the area defining the left side. Double-click to crop it. Export to GIF format.

16 Revert one more time and select the right side, crop, and export. Repeat this process for as many buttons as you need.

17 Create two versions for each button, one in back and one in front. Place the GIFs in a table in your HTML code, specifying <topmargin=0> and <leftmargin=0> to get the images to butt right up to the outside of the browser window. ■

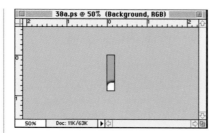

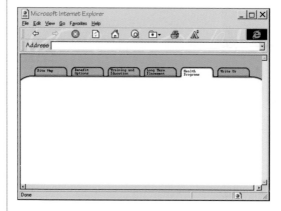

Buttons on Image

Incorporating navigational buttons into a photograph or existing artwork can transform almost any image into a useful interface. By combining Gaussian Blur with Brightness/Contrast adjustments, almost any part of the image can become a button.

1 Open your selected image. We used a photo from the Photo 24 Flowers and Leaves series. You could also use a custom texture.

2 Choose File➔Preferences➔ Guides & Grid (Gridline every 1", Subdivisions 3"). This gives you gridlines to create the buttons.

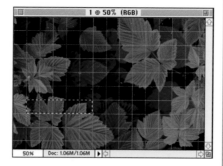

3 With the Marquee tool, select the area for your button. Save the selection (Channel #4).

4 Make Channel #4 active. Copy and paste the selection into the grid to create as many buttons as you want.

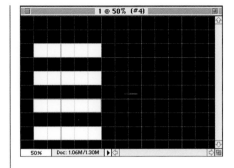

5 Return to the composite channel. Load the selection Channel #4.

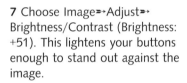

6 Choose Filter➡Blur➡Gaussian Blur (5.8 pixels). You can adjust the slider until you get the desired effect.

7 Choose Image➡Adjust➡ Brightness/Contrast (Brightness: +51). This lightens your buttons enough to stand out against the image.

8 Choose Edit➡Stroke (Width: 1 pixel, Location: Outside). We used the Eyedropper tool on the photo to select a complementary color for the stroke.

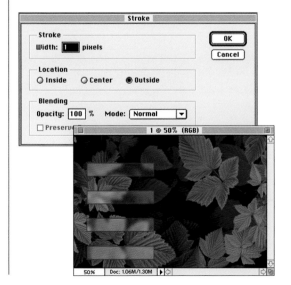

9 To finish the image, we added a drop shadow to the buttons (see Soft Shadows, page 72), and used Filter➡Blur➡Motion Blur (Angle: 45°, Distance: 60 pixels) as a variation to the Gaussian Blur filter. ■

Gradient Stripes

188

Matching image color precisely with background colors on your Web page is an important design consideration. One way of doing this is to use a 216-color no-dither palette optimized for the Web. Another way is to use a Color Picker utility to find a color's hexidecimal value for placement in your HTML document. After selecting a color, the Gradient tool offers a way to merge your graphics into a Web page's background.

Using several gradients across an image will blend the image into the background of your page, integrating the graphics into the Web page. It's important that you match the image color precisely with your background color—use a 216-color, non-dithering palette or a color picker utility to match colors. These tools can be found in the WebTools folder on the CD.

1 Choose an image to place over a color that will match the color of the background in your Web page. Select all and copy the image.

2 Create a new file that is larger than the image will be on the Web page (the New Image dialog box will reflect the current size of the image you have just copied. Add about an inch to the width and the height of the new image.) Paste the image. (This creates Layer 1.)

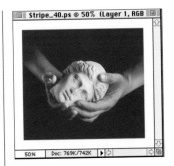

3 Choose a background color from the 216-color non-dithering palette a Color Picker utility (included on the CD in the WebTools folder) to define the hexadecimal values of the color. Fill the Background layer with the background color.

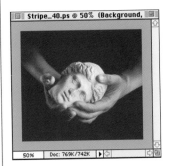

4 Choose View➡Show Grid. It's best if you either trim your photo with the Selection tool or edit your grid to fit the photo evenly. We used the grid default setting for this example.

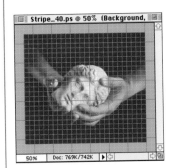

189

5 Use the Rectangular Marquee tool to make a vertical selection for the first gradient stripe. Continue to add horizontal selections by holding down the Shift key. Save the selection (Channel #4) in case you want to use it later. Choose View➡Hide grid.

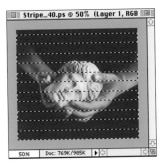

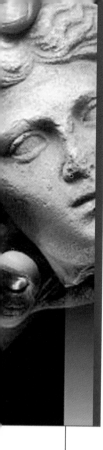

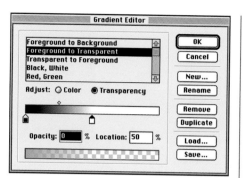

6 Switch Foreground/Background colors. Double-click the Gradient tool (Opacity: 100%, Gradient: Foreground to Transparent, Dither: off). Click the Edit Gradient button. Select the Transparency radio button and slide the Transparency icon (the right box) to Location: 50%.

7 Click directly under the far right end of the Transparency bar to add a color box at Location: 100%.

8 Drag the left diamond over the Transparency bar to Location: 30%. To expand the transparent area of the gradient, drag the right diamond to Location: 70%.

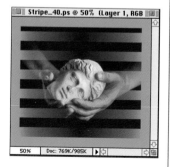

VARIATIONS

Here we added gradients to only one side of the image and added text to use the gradients as buttons.

 The possibilities of gradients are endless. Create your own library of gradients by saving new ones as Gradient presets and revising or deleting the ones you are not interested in. ■

White on White

Matching the color of the menu bar or text heading to the background has become a popular design style. The 3D effect is built by varying the hue and value in the shadow. Here we combine the Stroke feature with the Neon Glow filter to create a white-on-white menu bar.

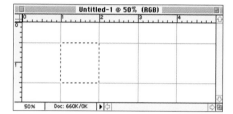

1 Create a new file (Width: 5 inches, Height 2 inches). Add vertical and horizontal guides. We placed vertical guides at each inch mark, and two horizontal guides a half inch from the top and bottom edges of the image area. With the Marquee tool select a rectangle corresponding to meeting points of the horizontal and vertical guides.

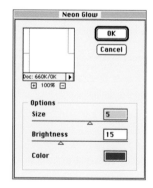

2 Create a new layer (Layer 1). Set the foreground color to white. Choose Edit➔Stroke (Width: 16 pixels, Location: Inside, Mode: Overlay). Because the Background is white, the effect will not be visible until the Neon Glow filter is applied.

3 Apply Filter➔Artistic➔Neon Glow. Choose the Move tool, hold down the Option [Alt] key and drag out four copies of the square.

4 After completing the five squares, use Steps 1 through 3 to create the upper and lower horizontal bars, but set the stroke width to 8 pixels.

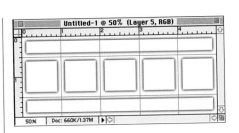

5 With the Type Mask tool, enter the text. We used Syntax Heavy, center alignment, anti-aliased on, spacing: 0. Use the Move tool to position the text. Add text to each of the buttons. Apply the same stroke as in Step 4 and the same neon glow as in Step 3.

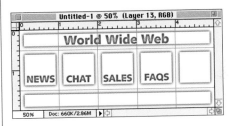

6 The word DEMO is too long for the box width. Choose Layer➡ Free Transform. Scale the text by moving tabs with cursor until it fits the box shape. Keep the same text height.

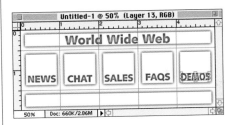

7 Repeat Step 5 to add text to the bottom bar. Flatten image. Export to GIF format.

193

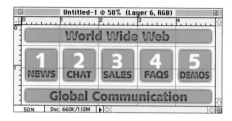

VARIATIONS

Changing the background to gray creates another possibility. After placing all text, merge all layers except the Background. Because the neon effect expands the width of the rectangular menu bars, there is no transparent space open except in the center of the shapes. When you change the background to gray, the new color will only fill the interior of the rectangular menu bars. Add additional text, such as numerals. ■

Cut Outs

While drop shadows are used to reinforce the visual illusion that objects are floating above the Web page, cutouts are the visual opposite, causing parts of the image to appear to recede into the page. Cutouts work well with objects that have drop shadows to further highlight and add interest to them.

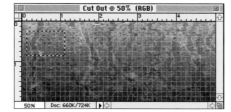

1 Open a file containing the texture you plan to use. In this example we used a marbleized texture, which you can find in the Web Magic folder on the CD-ROM. Choose View➭Show Grid. Use the guides to make a selection for your first button.

2 Save the selection (Channel #4). Make Channel #4 active. With the selection still active, copy and paste the new button selection. Repeat cut and paste until you have created all of your button selections, using the guidelines to align them. Return to the composite channel. Choose View➭Hide Grid.

3 Select➭All and copy the selection. Paste the selection, which will create a new layer (Layer 1). Load the selection Channel #4 and delete.

196

4 With Channel #4 still active make the background layer active. Choose Filter➔Gaussian Blur (2.0 pixels). Then choose Image➔ Adjust➔Brightness/Contrast (Brightness: +40, Contrast: -10).

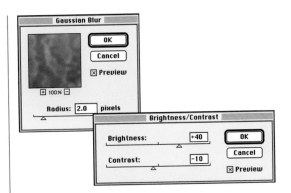

5 Choose Select➔None, then create a new layer (Layer 2) and fill it with black. Load the selection Channel #4 and delete.

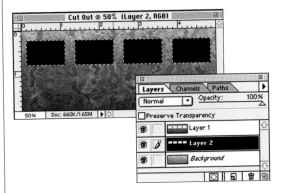

6 Select➔All and choose Filter➔ Gaussian Blur (6.0 pixels). With the Move tool, offset Layer 2 down and to the right to position the shadow in the upper-left edges of the buttons.

7 Create a new layer (Layer 3) and use the Type Mask tool to enter the text, then fill it with black. In this example we used the font Allise. Choose Image➔ Adjust➔Brightness/ Contrast (Brightness: -85, Contrast: +10).

8 Flatten the image and export to GIF format.

VARIATIONS

The cutout technique works great with type also. In Step 1, enter text with the Type Mask tool to make a selection. Save the selection (Channel #4) and continue with Steps 2 through 6. Flatten the image and export to GIF format.

Here we used a solid color for the cutout effect and added a beveled edge. Using the same color as the background of your Web page creates the illusion of the menu bar emerging from your background. ■

Duotones

Working with black-and-white photos on the Web, where everything is usually in full living color, can be a bit of a challenge. Changing an image to a duotone and using pattern filters jazzes up an otherwise dull photo. The final output for this exercise will be four separate images to be used as navigational buttons. Each image must match the others perfectly, so we'll make use of Photoshop 4.0's new guideline feature.

1 Open the image you will be using for this exercise. We used an image from Digital Stock, Inc.

2 We created four separate sections in the image by adding three horizontal guidelines over the image about $5/8$ of an inch apart, and one vertical guideline to ensure proper text alignment. If the rulers are not visible choose View➤Show Rulers.

3 Choose a foreground color and Enter your text using the solid Type tool.

4 To help define the text we added a drop shadow following the technique in Object Shadows. (See page 72).

5 Save the file as a Photoshop document(duotone.ps). Choose Image➟Mode➟Duotone (black and Pantone Red 032 CV).

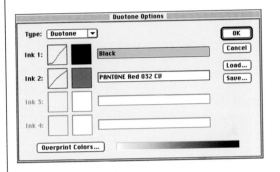

6 Work in Full Screen mode. With the Marquee tool, starting outside the image area, drag the marquee over the top section of the image and allow the selection to snap to the top horizontal guide. Make sure you have the "snap to guides" selected in the View drop-down menu.

7 Choose Image➟Edit➟Crop. This cuts away all but the top section of the image, which will be used as your first button. Choose Image➟Mode➟RGB, this will convert the image to RGB color allowing it to be exported to GIF89 format (name the file duotone1.gif).

201

8 Revert to the original image (duotone.ps) and repeat Steps 3 and 4 with the new type. Choose Image➟Mode➟Duotone and select a different color combination. We used black and a blue with RGB values 6, 6, 125.

9 Select the area between the second and third guidelines and let it snap to the guides. Choose Image➙Crop and export to GIF format (duotone2.gif) creating the second button for your Web site.

10 Repeat Step 3 through 7 for as many buttons as you'd like. We made four.

VARIATIONS

Duotone and Mezzotint

Working with the filters in Photoshop 4.0 can give you some interesting and varied effects. In our variation we used a combination of duotone and Mezzotint filters to create Web page buttons, which each have two versions. One to show an active link and one to show an inactive link. This variation actually works with two separate images that are cut and combined in different configurations inside the HTML document.

1 Choose: Pixelate➙Mezzotint➙ Small dots on the Grayscale image and save it as a new Photoshop document.

2 For the second image we created a duotone as described in Step 5 and saved that as a new Photoshop document.

3 We added type and different drop shadow effects to jazz up the image, then cut and saved the separate pieces of each image for use in the HTML document as buttons.

4 Use the different images to show which link you've connected to by highlighting that button and graying back the rest of the image. ■

PART VII

Animation

Animation is becoming an increasingly important aspect of Web page design. Seen as a welcome relief from pages of static HTML text, animation brings a fresh new energy to the conventional Web site.

Animation can be used to enhance pages or content themes. With greater frequency, companies are animating their Web advertising banners. The animation serves as the visual lure, enticing visitors to click the link to view the corporate message.

Animations do not need to be complex. Some of the best animations on the Web are small, discrete, and load quickly. Composed using a flip book technique, the animations are built with as few as two or three frames that may play once or loop continuously.

This series of individual frames can be created in Photoshop using the layers and actions palettes and the GIF89a format. When completed, the frames are then exported to software programs, such as GIF Builder or GIF Construction Set, for animating. In the following pages we demonstrate how to create some basic animation effects.

Rotate Animation

Rotating an object has always been fairly easy in Photoshop. Photoshop 4.0's Actions feature helps automate the process by allowing you to assign a single function key to a series of steps.

1 Create a new file or open an existing file containing a graphic for the animation. We used a stylized "O" from the decorative Crystal Balzac font in this example (included on the CD). If you are using an existing image, select the graphic. If you are creating a new image using text for this exercise when you create text with the Type tool, you are adding a layer to your document. The text appears on that new layer filled with the foreground color. Choose Layers➡Preserve Transparency.

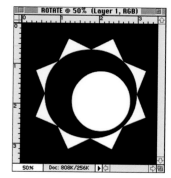

2 Select the Gradient tool and set the tool options to Opacity: 100%; Gradient: Blue, Red, Yellow; Type: linear.

Click the Edit button in the tool options panel and set the Red slider to 80%. You may want to save new gradient variations for the future by renaming them. Click and drag across your selection to define direction and length of gradation as shown in the figure.

3 Choose Windows➟Show Actions. Create a new action from the Actions Palette pop-up menu and name the action Rotate/Export. Assign a function key and a color and click the record button. From this point on all actions will be recorded to help automate the animation process.

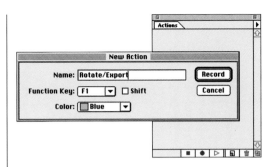

4 Choose Layer➟Transform➟ Numeric (Rotate: 36°).

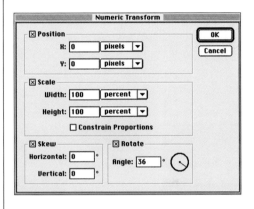

5 Export to GIF89a format and save the file.

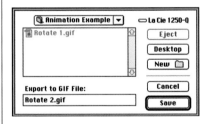

TIP By using the function key assigned to these steps, you create a series of files. When naming these files, give them sequential names (rotate1.gif, rotate2.gif, rotate3.gif and so on).

6 Return to the Actions dialog box and stop recording the Action (in the Actions Palette pop-up menu).

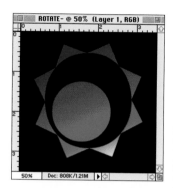

7 Use the function key you designated to create the rest of the GIFs for the animation.

Save the entire sequence in its own folder as you export it. This makes opening and importing into your animation program easier.

After you have all the individual files for your rotation, you are ready to import them into GifBuilder (Macintosh), Gif Construction Set (Windows), or another animation program.

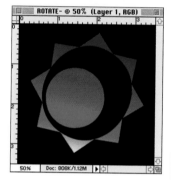

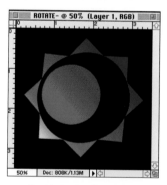

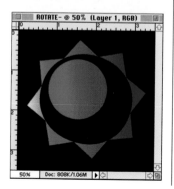

VARIATIONS

In this example we rotate only the beveled edge of this button. The bevel rotation requires only four steps and creates a good-looking rotating button effect. Instead of rotating the image 36° as in the previous exercise, this button requires only four 90° rotations. The text was pasted into the center of each image after it was rotated. ■

Fade On/Off Animation

The Gaussian Blur filter can be used repeatedly on images to create an excellent fade effect. Each time the Gaussian Blur is applied, the image spreads and appears lighter. This process is used to make objects appear to disappear or (if placed in reverse order in an animation program) to fade-up and appear.

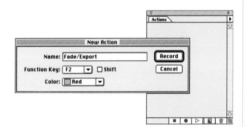

1 Create a new file or open an existing file containing the image you are using for the animation. Remember to allow enough space (approximately 1/2 inch or more) around the entire image for the fade to spread as it gets lighter. Choose Select➔All.

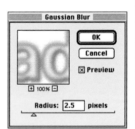

2 Create a new action called Fade/Export. Choose a function key for your new action. Click the record button.

3 Choose Filter➔Blur➔Gaussian Blur (2.5 pixels). A higher blur number will require fewer animation steps.

4 Export to GIF format. Name the GIFs sequentially (fade1.gif, fade 2.gif, fade3.gif and so on) and save them in their own folder as you export it. The example in this exercise requires seven steps to fully fade. The number of steps required varies depending on the image and the setting you choose for the Gaussian Blur.

5 Return to the Action dialog box and stop recording the Action (In the Actions Palette pop-up menu).

The action has now been recorded and you can use the function key you designated to create the rest of the GIFs for the animation. (If you have a keyboard without function keys, you can highlight the action in the palette and press play at the bottom of the palette or use the Action palette's pop-up menu to view the palette in Button mode.

6 When you play this action a Gaussian blur is automatically applied to your image, the GIF89a Export dialog box appears, and, when you click OK, a Save dialog box appears where you can name your new GIF. Successive blurs produce a full fade effect. Continue this process until you have faded your image as desired.

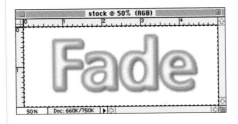

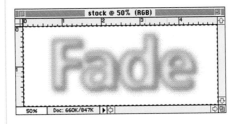

7 Save your last file as an empty frame for full fade-out effect. After you have all the individual rotation images you are ready to import them into GifBuilder (Macintosh), GIF Construction Set (Windows), or another animation program.

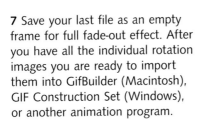

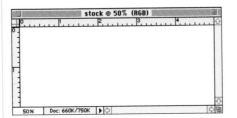

211

TIP As you create the different steps of an animation, you might want to alter the pace of the motion (in the preceding example, for example, you might want to increase the rate of fade). To do this, select the step of the action you want to change, then choose Record Again in the Action options pop-up menu. The Record Again command reflects the option you selected (in our example the palette command is Record "Gaussian Blur" Again). At this point you can add a custom setting. ▪

Write-On Animation

This exercise illustrates an animation that writes a word one letter at a time from left to right. This simple technique requires the creation of sequential images with a new letter added to each one. The final effect is similar to type applied by a typewriter.

1 Open a copy of an existing file containing the type for the animation. For this exercise we used the Jasper type face with a chrome effect.

TIP Animation programs such as GifBuilder, Gif Construction Set, and others offer many features for image manipulation and animation such as image offset, interframe delay, and palette control. Some Web-based animation programs even contain more advanced functions such as morphing.

2 Use the Crop tool from the Marquee pop-up menu to drag a selection around the image. When you are satisfied with the selection, press Return/Enter to crop. This keeps the file sizes small. Note: For illustration purposes we did not crop our artwork tightly.

3 Create a new layer (Layer 1) and use the Marquee tool (or lasso) to select the portion of the image that will *not* appear in the first frame of the animation. Choose Edit➤Fill➤ (Use: White, Opacity: 100%, Mode: Normal). Save a copy of this image as a protection just in case you make a mistake and write over the original file.

4 Export as a GIF. Give the GIF a sequential name such as letter1.gif, letter2.gif, letter3.gif, and so on.

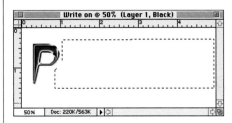

5 Make Layer 1 active. Use the Move tool to drag the white box on Layer 1 to reveal the characters that appear in the second frame of the animation. Hold the Shift key down to constrain the motion horizontally. Export as a GIF.

6 Repeat Step 5 until you have exported a GIF for each letter.

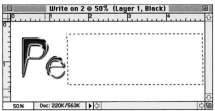

215

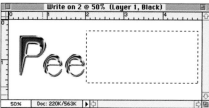

VARIATIONS

You don't have to use letters as the units for this effect. Here we used circular selections to create a different effect.

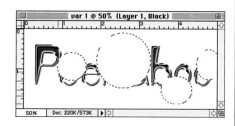

We created this colorful variation by using Image➛Adjust➛Color Balance and changing the settings for each frame. ■

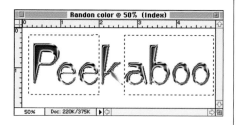

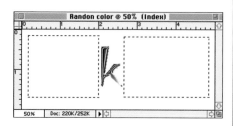

Three Step Marquee

Chaser lights flashing around movie marquees, in carnivals, and other entertainment venues have been used traditionally to add flash and fanfare. The marquee effect of flashing lights framing an image can be achieved with only three frames of animation giving that exciting carnival effect of moving lights.

1 Create a new file. Select a round brush and open the Brush Options dialog box and set the Spacing to 130%. Using Photoshop's brush options you can set any brush to create uniform lines of shapes.

TIP Any setting over 100% will separate the brush strokes and enable you to use it as a repeating pattern line. A round brush will create a line of bullets.

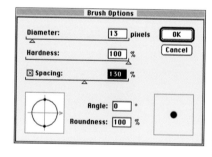

2 Use the modified brush with the Paintbrush tool to draw a horizontal line creating a line of bullet points. With the Marquee tool select three bullet points. Keep the selection tight to the bullets.

TIP Press the Command key to access the Move tool when another tool is active. Holding down the Option key when you drag a selection with the Move tool will create a copy of the selection. Holding down the Shift key as you drag constrains the drag horizontally, vertically or 45° diagonally.

3 Choose Edit➥Define Pattern. Then create a new file (we chose 250 pixels high×450 pixels wide for this example). Choose Edit➔ Fill➔Pattern. You will wind up with broken bullets along some of the edges, Don't worry, just delete any broken bullets first to clean up the edges of your image.

4 After any broken bullets are deleted, you will have a clean edge of solid bullets around the parameter of your image. You want to end up with a rectangular box defined by a single line of solid bullet points. You'll need to place your Marquee tool just inside the first outside row of bullets. Select all the bullets inside the outer row of bullets except those on the outer edges, as shown in the figure.

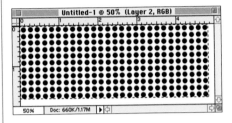

5 Delete the selection. You're left with an even border of bullets that will be the base for your marquee. With the Magic Wand tool select one of the black bullets and choose Select➔Similar. Save the selection. After the selection is saved, select All, Edit➔Fill➔Black, creating a black background.

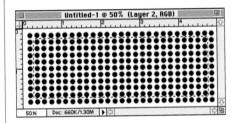

When you save a selection, you are creating a channel. Every time you save a selection an additional channel is added. If you are working in RGB, the first selection saved is named Channel #4. If you are working in CMYK, the first selection you save is named Channel #5. Just as you can customize the names of layers, you can also change the names of channels. If you are saving multiple selections, it will make life a lot easier if you give specific names to

channels. Also bear in mind that every time you save a selection you are adding another 8-bit brightness channel to your document and the size of your document will increase accordingly. It is a good idea to delete unnecessary channels.

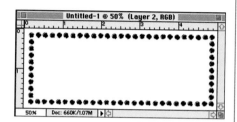

6 Create a new layer (Layer 1) and load selection (#4). Choose Select➤Modify➤Expand (2 pixels). From the Window Menu choose show swatches, place your pointer over the yellow square in the first row of color swatches and click on it. Choose Edit➤Fill➤Foreground color. Duplicate the new layer 2 times. You will now have 3 layers and the *Background*.

7 Create a new layer (Layer 4), load the selection. Choose Edit➤ Fill (Use: White).

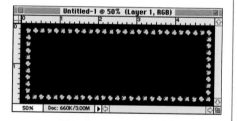

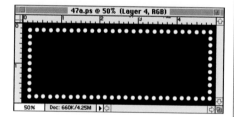

8 To create the glowing light effect around the light, Make Layer 1 active, Option-click on the eye icon to hide the other layers, and use the Magic Wand tool and the Shift key to select every third bullet. Choose Select➤Inverse and delete. Then Press Command-A (select all) and choose Filter➤ Gaussian Blur (5 pixels).

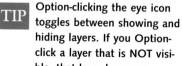

Option-clicking the eye icon toggles between showing and hiding layers. If you Option-click a layer that is NOT visible, that layer becomes visible and the other layers are hidden. You still, however-er, need to click the layer name in the palette to make it active.

9 Make Layer 2 active and repeat Step 8 moving one bullet to the right from the one place you started on Layer 1. Make sure you're always selecting the bullet to the right of the one you deleted on Layer 1. Repeat this process with Layer 3.

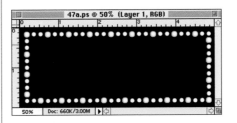

10 Create a new layer (Layer 5) and place any type or other images that need to be present in the marquee. If you are creating type in this document, do NOT make a new layer. Simply select the Type tool and create the text— in Photoshop 4.0, text created with the Type tool comes in on a new layer. In this example we added the word Marquee.... Using Layer 5 keeps the versions you save consistent so that only the "lights" of the marquee appear to be moving.

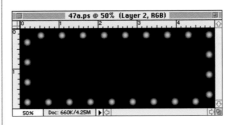

11 Make the background, Layer 1, Layer 4, and Layer 5 visible and export to GIF format.

12 Make Layers 2, 4 and 5 visible and export to GIF format.

Repeat Step 12 one more time, this time using Layers 3, 4, and 5, creating a total of three GIFs.

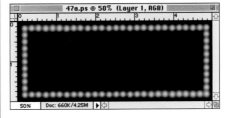

TIP You can now import the files into GifBuilder (Macintosh), GIF Construction Set (Windows) or another animation program to create the final animation.

221

VARIATION

This variation makes the lights chase around the frame, pause, flash on and off, and then go back to chasing.

1 Open your original Photoshop document and make all three layers of the blurred yellow bullets visible, hiding the text layer (Layer 5) and the layer with the white bullets (Layer 4). Export to GIF format.

2 Return to the original document and make the background, Layer 4, and Layer 5 visible. Export to GIF format.

3 In your GIF animation program, insert the GIF from Step 2 after the original three GIFs. Insert the GIF from Step 1, followed by the GIF from Step 2 again, and then repeat the series of the first three GIFs in reverse order. ■

TOOLBOX

KPT Texture
Explorer

Twirl Animation

Twisted or twirled animation effects are easier to do with Photoshop 4.0 and its new Actions palette because you can record every step of a sequential action and save it. In this exercise we combined the Twirl filter with Transform to create an animation that spins and shrinks at the same time.

1 Create a new file (Background: white) and select the Ellipse marquee tool. Select a circular area.

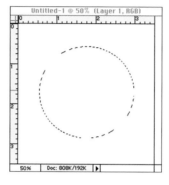

TIP Keep animated GIFs fairly small. As you design your animation, keep in mind that because it is a local file, the animation runs as fast as your computer can play it. When it is viewed the final animation plays only as fast as the animation file loads on a Web page (usually 14.4 or 28.8 Kbs). It is only after the file is finished loading that it will run as fast as it is programmed to run.

2 Choose Selection Menu➤Feather (15 pixels). Fill with your pattern or texture. We used a texture from MetaTools KPT Texture Explorer for this example. You can also use an existing texture file: Open the file containing the texture you want to use. Select all and choose Edit➤Define Pattern. Return to the original file and with the feathered selection still selected choose Edit➤Fill➤(Use: Pattern).

3 For the button in the center of the twirl, create a new layer (Layer #1). Select a rectangular area and Edit➔Fill➔Foreground (White, Opacity: 80%).

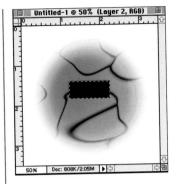

4 With the rectangle still selected, create a new layer (Layer 2). Choose a foreground color for the button and fill a selection with the foreground color. We then added a bevel using the Alien Skin Inner Bevel filter. Return to Layer 1, select the Move tool, and use the arrow keys to move it down and to the right to create a drop shadow.

5 Use the Type tool to add type to the button. This creates a new Layer (Layer 3). Choose a Foreground color for the type.

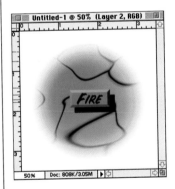

225

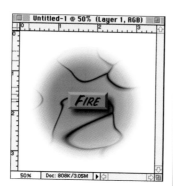

6 To soften the drop shadow, keep Layer 1 active and apply Filter➟Blur➟Gaussian Blur (3 pixels). Save the file as a Photoshop document, naming it "base.gif" and export it as a GIF89a.

7 Now we'll apply the twirl effect. Open the Actions palette and choose Window➟Show Actions. Create a new action. Name the action and assign a function key and color for the button. Click Record. Every action you take will be recorded and saved for future use.

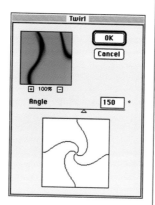

8 Select➟All, make the background layer active, and then choose Filter➟Distort➟Twirl (150°).

9 Export the image as a GIF89a file. Name it twirl1.gif.

10 Click the stop button on the Actions palette.

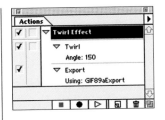

11 Click Play on your Actions palette. The image is rotated an additional 150°. When the export dialog box appears, name the image twirl2.gif and save it in the same folder as the rest of your images.

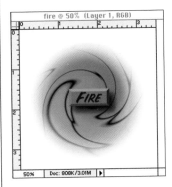

12 Repeat Step 11 two more times, naming the GIFs sequentially (twirl3.gif, twirl4.gif).

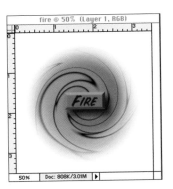

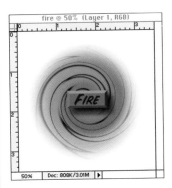

227

fire @ 50% (Layer 1, RGB)
50% Doc: 808K/3.01M

13 Creating the twirl in the opposite direction follows the same process, entering a negative number in the Twirl dialog box. Revert to the file saved in Step 5. On the Actions palette select the Twirl action. From the Actions palette's pop-up menu choose Record Twirl Again. Enter -150° in the Twirl dialog box. Export the file to GIF format (twirl5.gif).

fire @ 50% (Layer 1, RGB)
50% Doc: 808K/3.01M

14 The action is now modified to twirl in the opposite direction. Repeat the action 3 more times, as above in Step 12, to create the additional GIFs.

15 You are now ready to bring the GIF sequence into an animation program such as GifBuilder or Gif Construction Set. Arrange the GIFs in the following order: base, twirl1.gif, twirl2.gif, twirl3.gif, twirl4.gif, twirl3.gif, twirl2.gif, twirl1.gif, base.gif, twirl5.gif, twirl6.gif, twirl7.gif, twirl8.gif, twirl7.gif, twirl6.gif, twirl5.gif. Set the animation to loop forever and you will have an animation that twirls to the right and unwinds, then to the left and unwinds.

fire @ 50% (Layer 1, RGB)
50% Doc: 808K/3.01M

fire @ 50% (Layer 1, RGB)
50% Doc: 808K/3.01M

VARIATION

Shrinking Twirl

This variation combines two Photoshop effects, twirl and numeric transform, into each Action step, creating an effect that shrinks and grows as it twirls.

In this exercise we added two additional steps to the action: Numeric Transform to shrink the graphic and a Revert command to bring you back to the original file (The Revert is necessary to make the Numeric Transform work smoothly). Because we are reverting after each step, you have to enter the values manually into the Twirl and Transform dialog boxes.

1 Follow Steps 1-5 to create the base image for the animation. In this example we made an open frame instead of a solid button.

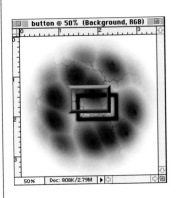

2 Make the background layer active and Select➔All. Create a new action. Name the action, make a function key assignment, and select a color for the action button. Press Record on the Actions palette to begin recording. Choose Filter➔Distort➔Twirl (100°), then choose Layers➔Transform➔Numeric (Scale: Horiz: 90, Vert: 90). Next, choose

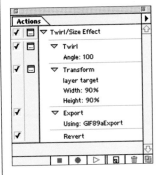

File➡Export as GIF89a, name the GIF, and choose File➡Revert.

3 To the left of the action commands on the Actions palette are break point check boxes (containing an icon of a dialog box). Select the boxes next to your actions. The Toggle option causes the action to pause at the dialog box of each element of your action, waiting for input.

4 With each execution of the action, increase the Twirl value by 100° and reduce the Numeric Transform tool Scale by 10%.

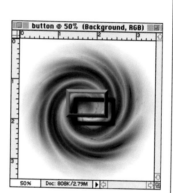

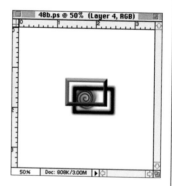

5 Repeat the process until the textured twirl almost disappears behind the button, this should take eight or nine steps. ■

Using GifBuilder

GifBuilder is a Mac-only freeware utility from Yves Piguet designed for creating animated GIF files. You can use an existing animated GIF, a group of PICT, GIF and TIFF files, or a QuickTime movie. GifBuilder will output these file formats as a GIF89a file with multiple pages, creating an animation that you can use on the Web.

GifBuilder is a user-friendly program which provides many options. These include interlacing, color palettes, pixel depth, dithering, image size, background color, looping, transparency, frame offset, interframe delay, disposal method and saving options.

This exercise will demonstrate only the basics of GifBuilder touching upon looping, and interframe delay. You can find the program in the Web Tools folder. For further information on how GifBuilder works refer to the documentation provided with the program.

1 Open GifBuilder.

2 Choose File➔Add Frame (Command-K) and add each GIF file for the animation.

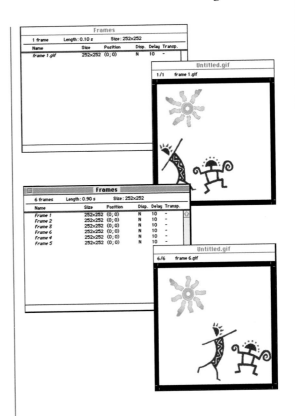

TIP **Always save your original animation files in alphabetical or numerical order, that is, 1ani.gif, 2ani.gif, and so on. GifBuilder will then open and place the frames in the correct order.**

3 Choose Animation➔Start (Command-R) to play your animation. If you want to rearrange your frames, select the frame. As you drag the frame, a guideline will appear. Place the guideline where you would like the frame placed.

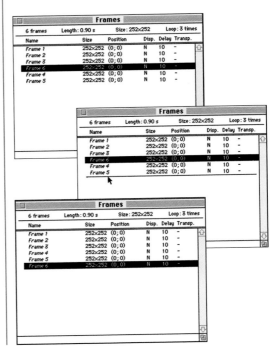

233

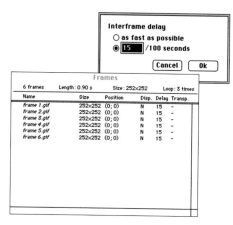

4 Choose Options➡Loop. Using the looping dialog box loop your graphic as desired. You can set the animation to play once, any number of times, or forever. For this exercise we looped it 3 times.

5 To adjust timing between frames, choose Options➡ Interframe delay (or double-click the number display in the Delay column on the Frames window). Set the time for each frame. For this exercise we chose 15. The delay time can vary from frame to frame for special effects.

6 Choose File➡Save as. You can now place the finished GIF animation on a Web page as you would any other GIF. To view this animation open gb1.gif (in the Animation Examples folder on the CD-ROM) in GifBuilder or a Web browser.

VARIATIONS

Looping Animations

By duplicating selected frames, we created a smooth looping effect.

Select all frames except the first and last. Use Command-D to duplicate the selected frames, then arrange the duplicated frames in reverse order. This will create a smooth continuous loop effect.

To view this animation open gb2.gif (in the Animation Examples folder on the CD-ROM) in GifBuilder or a Web browser.

Delaying and Duplicating Frames

This variation demonstrates inter-frame delay and duplicate frame effects. Changing the delay to 20 and duplicating frames 3 and 4 creates a pause and dancing effect with the figures in mid-animations.

To view this animation open gb3.gif (in the Animation Examples folder on the CD-ROM) in GifBuilder or a Web browser. ■

GIF Construction Set

To create animations for the Web you need an animation program. The GIF Construction Set from Alchemy Mindworks is a simple to use shareware program for Windows that can be downloaded from www.mindworkshop.com. You work with dialog boxes that takes you step by step through the process for creating animated GIFs for the Web.

1 Open the program and select the Animation Wizard from the File menu to start the automation process.

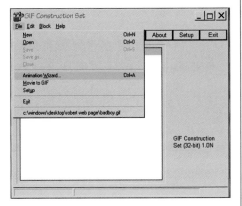

2 Follow the instructions on the different dialog boxes and the program will take you through each step, asking you several questions about the type of animation you want to create. Make sure you select the option "For use on the World Wide Web".

3 Next the program requests that you enter delay time between screens measured in hundredths of seconds.

4 Locate the GIF files included in the animation. The program compiles an animated GIF file including the images in your sequence.

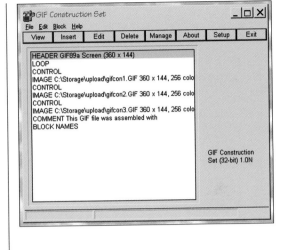

5 Click View to see the animation in action. You can change or edit the animation with GIF Construction Set's easy-to-use buttons bar. You can alter the speed, looping effects, and even insert or reorder frames.

6 When you are pleased with the way the animation works, save it as a GIF file. Place the animated GIF into your Web page just like a standard GIF file:

```
<IMG SCR="xx.gif" WIDTH="xx"
HEIGHT="xx" ALT="animated
gif"> ■
```

Appendix A

Web Resources Links

HTML pages containing these links can be found in the WebMagic folder on the CD.

Information SuperLibrary

http://www.mcp.com

Viacom's Information SuperLibrary contains the complete text of The Internet Starter Kit (both Windows and Mac versions). Overall the site contains the depth of information you would expect from the world's largest publisher of computer books.

Dodd's Magic Locator

http://www.netdepot.com/~gargoyle/magic/links.html

Photoshop Web Magic's favorite link to magic on the Web. A great gateway site to magicians, magazines, organizations, retailers, news, and just about anything else on magic.

Photoshop Resources

Adobe

http://www.adobe.com

The Adobe site contains continuing product support information, Photoshop and design tips, updates, plug-ins and other up to date information.

Adobe Plug-In Source Catalog

http://www.imageclub.com/aps/

The Adobe Plug-in Source is a comprehensive software catalog that brings the power of plug-ins to your workstation.

The KPT Photoshop Forum

http://the-tech.mit.edu/cgi-bin/HyperNews/get/KPT/pshop.html

This ongoing forum is for any questions or discussion about using Adobe Photoshop and any of its third party add-ins.

Photoshop Web Magic

216 Colors of Netscape

`http://www.connect.hawaii.com/hc/webmasters/Netscape.colors.html`

This is the place to learn about using the 216-color Safe Palette on the Web.

Metatools—KPT Plug-ins

`http://www.metatools.com`

The developers of Kai Power Tools and other very cool graphics software.

PNG (Portable Network Graphics) Home Page

`http://quest.jpl.nasa.gov/PNG/"`

Find out more about the PNG graphic format here.

Pantone: What's New

`http://www.pantone.com/whatsnew.html`

A great place for color resources, information, and software.

Design Resources

Designers Guide to the Net

`http://www.zender.com/designers-guide-net`

This site, and the book it is based on, attempts to raise the right questions, and propose answers that will help designers in the information future.

Pursuing Page Publishing

`http://www.links.net/webpub/`

Tips on "Publish yo' self" at this site. Includes a guide to designing with HTML and links to many other Web resources.

Cybergrrl

`http://www.cybergrrl.com`

Author of Designing Web Graphics, Lynda Weinman's Cybergrrl site can help guide you through getting started on the Web, offer HTML instruction, link you to important Web sites, and lots more.

Web Wonk—Tips for Writers and Designers

`http://www.dsiegel.com/tips/index.html`

Web Wonk by David Siegel, author of *Building Killer Web Sites*, will help you to build better Web pages, use email, and offers great tips on Web site graphic design.

Tom's Tips for Web Designers

`http://www.the-tech.mit.edu/KPT/Toms/index.html`

Find all kinds of Photoshop tips here including: Web design, using filters, and links to other resources.

Ventana: Photoshop f/x

`http://www.vmedia.com/vvc/onlcomp/phshpfx/`

This site is based on the book Photoshop f/x, lots of design tips, and links to Photoshop resources.

Yahoo Design and Layout

`http://www.yahoo.com/Computers_and_Internet/Internet/World_Wide_Web/Page_`
`➡Design_and_Layout`

This Yahoo category is as up to date and comprehensive as it gets. It includes links to Animated GIFs, Backgrounds, Color Information, Commercial Books, Commercial Web Page, Designers, HTML, Icons, Imagemaps, Programming, Transparent Images, and Validation/Check.

Backgrounds

Texture Land—Abnormal Textures Index

`http://www.meat.com/textures/aindex.html`

This site offers one of the largest selections of backgrounds on the Web.

KALEIDESCAPE

`http://www.steveconley.com/kaleid.htm`

This site claims to offer "hundreds of the snazziest textures in the universe."

Textures Unlimited!

`http://www.smoky.org/~bzhuk/texture/f-1.html`

Click on a texture at this site and it automatically shows you what the tile looks like when applied to a Web page. There are some flashy textures here and music clips to download.

Photoshop Web Magic

Greg's Texture Tiles Page

http://mars.ark.com/~gschorno/tiles/

Find lots of tiles here in a simple table-based layout.

The Background Sampler

http://www.netscape.com/assist/net_sites/bg/backgrounds.html

Netscape's collection of backgrounds. Lots of basic textures and standard patterns here.

The Wallpaper Machine

http://www.cacr.caltech.edu/cgi-bin/wallpaper.pl

This interactive page makes funky random background patterns each time you click reload.

Netscape—Color Backgrounds

http://home.netscape.com/assist/net_sites/bg/

Netscape's instruction page on using background color with HTML3.

InfiNet's background colors list

http://www.infi.net/wwwimages/colorindex.html

Information on setting and using hex color for Web page backgrounds and text.

Type on the Web

TypoGraphic

http://www.razorfish.com/bluedot/typo/

"This site is meant to illustrate the beauty, poetry, complexity, and history of type, while raising relevant questions about how typography is treated in the digital media, specifically online."

DesktopPublishing.com

http://desktoppublishing.com/

Lots of fonts, images, and links to a wide range of design and programming resources.

Type Directors Club

http://members.aol.com/typeclub/index.html

An organization dedicated to the appreciation and understanding of letterforms and calligraphy.

BitStream Fonts

http://www2.digitalriver.com/bit/index.html

Over 1,000 fonts for sale online.

Letraset

http://www.letraset.com/letraset/

Download a free sample font, review new fonts, plus clip art and stock photography.

Coolfont

http://members.aol.com/fontdude/coolfont.htm

If you are into grunge and other trendy types of fonts Fontdude's site offers a great collection for a modest fee.

Buttons On the Web

Welcome to the WebTools Home Page

http://www.artbeatswebtools.com/frdoor.html

Artbeats WebTools is a CD-ROM containing hundreds of Web page elements: buttons, headings, rules, and so on. Download sample images here.

Download Free Clipart

http://www.sausage.com/clipart.htm

The folks at Sausage Software, makers of the Hot Dog Pro HTML editor, offer some very nice textures, clip art, and buttons for your pages.

Button World

http://www.demon.co.uk/Tangent/buttons.html

Button World is a collection of blank buttons, each one is optimized for rapid transmission over the Internet. Add text to these buttons and use them on your web pages.

Clip Art on the Web

Doubleexposure Homepage Starter Kit

http://www.doubleexposure.com

Photoshop Web Magic

Icons, buttons, clip art—order collections from this site or download and use some of the sample images they offer.

Metatools - Metatoys

`http://metatoys.metatools.com`

Search through over 2,200 images from the Power Photos and MetaPhotos collections online, then purchase and download just the images you want for immediate use.

Publishers Depot

`http://www.publishersdepot.com/`

This site calls itself a one-stop site for digital photography, fonts, video, and audio. It pretty much lives up to its claim with thousands of images and resources to choose from.

Photodisc

`http://www.photodisc.com/`

Simply the largest collection of royalty free, digital stock photography on the Internet.

Animation Resources

Gallery of GIF Animation

`http://www.reiworld.com/royalef/galframe.htm`

This is one of the best starting points for information on GIF animation resources, samples, and technical information.

Java Resources

`http://studwww.rug.ac.be/~vwillems/JAVA/`

Java samples, animations, and lots of links and resources.

The Web Getting Started

CERN—Where the Web was Developed

`http://www.cern.ch/`

CERN, European Laboratory for Particle Physics, this is where the Web was developed. CERN's Expert support: The WWW Support Team runs the main WWW server at CERN and gives general support to WWW information.

The World Wide Web Consortium

`http://www.w3.org/hypertext/WWW/`

W3C is an industry consortium which develops common standards for the evolution of the Web by producing specifications and reference software.

InterNIC Domain Registration Services

`http://www.internic.net`

The InterNIC is the primary source for domain registration. You can do a search here for names that aren't already taken.

The List (Internet Service Providers)

`http://www.thelist.com/`

Get information on over 3,000 ISPs, Internet Service Providers. Listed geographically and by area code.

c/net Guide to ISPs

`http://www.cnet.com/Content/Reviews/Compare/ISP/`

Tips on how to choose an ISP along with vital statistics on national and local ISPs. Find out which ISPs live up to their claims, and which you should be wary of until they clean up their act.

WPD—Magazine Rack

`http://www.littleblue.com/webpro/magazinerack.html`

The Web Professionals' Digest—Magazine Rack links you to over 75 Web based, Web focused magazines.

A Beginners Guide to URLs

`http://shemp.ncsa.uiuc.edu/NCSA/Staff/SDG/TESTER/Experimental/demoweb/url-primer.html"`

What is a URL? A URL is a Uniform Resource Locator. This beginner's guide offers a quick walk through of some of the more common URL types and how to use them.

Beginners Guide to HTML

`http://www.ncsa.uiuc.edu/General/Internet/WWW/HTMLPrimer.html`

This is the most requested page on the National Center for Supercomputing Applications (NCSA) Web site. If you are interested in learning HTML this is the starting point.

Photoshop Web Magic

Glenn's Cheat Sheet on HTML Style

`http://info.med.yale.edu/caim/StyleManual_Top.HTML`

Learn HTML directly from Yale's Center for Advanced Instructional Media. This site contains concise HTML instructions and tips.

Submit It

`http://submit-it.permalink.com/submit-it/`

Once you have your site up on the Web you will need to get it listed on search engines, and so on. One of the best places to do this is at Submit it.

Web Resources

Shareware.com

`http://www.shareware.com`

If it's shareware you can find it here. Over 200,000 searchable, downloadable software files.

Bandwidth Conservation Society

`http://www.infohiway.com/faster`

This site is a resource to help Web page designers with an interest in optimizing performance, but still maintaining an appropriate graphic standard. Information on file formats, links to Java applets, and more.

BrowserWatch

`http://browserwatch.iworld.com`

Go to this site to keep up on the latest news on browsers, plug-ins, and other Web resources.

Web trends

`http://www.interse.com/webtrends/`

Keep track of which browsers are being used on the Web. This site tracks and graphs browser usage.

EFF—The Electronic Frontier Foundation

`http://www.eff.org/`

The EFF is an important organization helping to keep the Web free from censorship.

JavaWorld—Java Jumps

`http://www.javaworld.com/common/jw-jumps.html`

JavaWorlds—Java Jumps this is a comprehensive collection of links to Java resources, collections, tools, and so on.

The VRML Repository

`http://sdsc.edu/vrml`

The VRML Repository is an impartial, comprehensive, community resource for the dissemination of information relating to VRML. Maintained by the San Diego Supercomputer Center (SDSC).

The Perl Language Home Page

`http://www.perl.com/perl/index.html`

Learn about Perl a common CGI language, with over 5,000 Perl resources and CGI's.

CGI Test Cases

`http://hoohoo.ncsa.uiuc.edu/cgi/examples.html`

A collection of CGI's to add forms, animation, functionality, and more to your Web pages.

Appendix B

Contributors Listing

For more information on the software, filters, fonts, stock photography, and textures we used to create our Web graphics, please contact the following companies.

Fonts

International Typeface Corporation

228 East 45th Street - 12th floor

New York, New York 10017

voice: 212/949-8072

fax: 212/949-8485

itc@esselte.com or typeface@aol.com

Software and Filters

Adobe Systems, Inc.

345 Park Avenue

San Jose, CA 95110-2704

voice: 408/536-6000

      800/833-6687

fax: 408/537-6000

http://www.adobe.com

Alien Skin Software

1100 Wake Forest Rd., Suite 101

Raleigh, NC 27604

voice: 919/832-4124

fax: 919/832-4065

alien-skin@alienskin.com

Equilibrium

Three Harbor Drive - Suite 111

Sausalito, CA 94965

voice: 415/332-4343

    800/524-8651

fax: 415/332-4433

http://www.equilibrium.com

Equilibrium DeBabelizer® Lite LE $59.00 value—Free!

Yves Piguet

http://iawww.epfl.ch/Staff/Yves.Piguet/

mailto:piguet@ia.epfl.ch

MetaTools

6303 Carpinteria Avenue

Carpinteria, CA 93013

voice: 805/566-6200

    800/472-9025

fax: 805/566-6385

KPTSupport@aol.com

Naoto Arakawa

GCA00443@niftyserve.or.jp

Specular International

7 Pomeroy Lane

Amherst, MA 01002

voice: 413/253-3100

fax: 413/253-0540

http://www.specular.com

Xaos Tools Inc.

600 Townsend St. - Suite 270 East

San Francisco, CA 94103

voice: 415/487-7000

      800/289-9267

fax: 415/558-9886

macinfo@xaostools.com

Stock Imagery & Textures
Digital Stock

400 South Sierra Avenue - Suite 100

Solana Beach, CA 92075-2262

voice: 619/794-4040

      800/545-4514

fax: 619/794-4041

http://www.digitalstock.com

D'Pix

A Division of Amber Productions, Inc.

414 West Fourth Avenue

PO Box 572

Columbus, OH 43216-0572

voice: 614/299-7192

fax: 614/294-0002

email:amber@infinet.com

251

Photoshop Web Magic

Image Club Graphics

A Division of Adobe Systems Inc.

729 Twenty-Fourth Ave. SE

Calgary, AB CANADA

T2G 5K8

voice: 403/262-8008

  800/661-9410

fax: 403/261-7013

http://www.imageclub.com

Used with express permission. Adobe® and Image Club Graphics™ are trademarks of Adobe Systems Incorporated.

Jawai Interactive

401 East Fourth St. #443

Austin, TX 78701-3745

voice: 512/469-0502

fax: 512/469-7850

http://www.jawai.com or sales @jawai.com

PHOTO 24 Texture Resource

7948 Faust Avenue

West Hills, CA 91304

voice: 818/999-4184

  800/582-9492 outside CA

fax: 818/999-5704

http://www.photo24.com (effective 1/1/97)

PhotoDisc, Inc.

2013 Fourth Avenue - 4th floor

Seattle, WA 98121

voice: 206/441-9355

  800/528-3472

fax: 206/441-9379

`http://www.photodisc.com`

Production Note

During this book project we used an EPSON Stylus ProXL color ink jet printer and an EPSON ES-1200C scanner.

Some images provided by Digital Stock, D'Pix, Image Club Graphics, Meta Tools, PHOTO 24 and PhotoDisc, 1996.

Some fonts provided by ITC and URW, 1996.

253

Appendix C

What's on the CD-ROM

The CD-ROM that comes with this book is both Macintosh and Windows compatible. Please note: There are several demos and tryouts available for Macintosh users that are not available for Windows users, and vice versa. This means one of two things: either the product has not been created for that platform, or a version of the product is being created but is not yet completed.

We suggest that you refer to the READ ME and other information files included in the demo software program's folder. Also, visit the corporate Web sites; the URLs are noted in the Contributors Listing (Appendix B). There are often demos of new software available for downloading and tryout.

Contents

The CD-ROM is divided into seven folders:

WebMagic This is a collection of ready-to-use files which we created for use with the tutorials. Open this folder, when you need to refer to these files to complete an exercise. Inside the WebMagic folder are several folders. You can use the links.html file to set up our Bookmarks list on your computer for easy Web browsing.

WebTools This is a collection of programs that will help you to be more productive when you build your Web graphics.

Effects You can use this collection of effects for manipulating images in Photoshop. Featured are a backgrounds and border sampler from ITC (International Typeface Corporation) and an Acrobat PDF file describing the new products from Auto F/X.

Filters Within this folder are freeware, some shareware and some commercial demos of popular filters. You can use these filters to modify and change your images into totally new looks. Experiment, have fun. This is where Photoshop helps you to release your creative potential.

Fonts Here we have a sample of fonts from ITC, a recognized leader in typeface design and innovation.

Photoshop Web Magic

Images We include a collection of 72 dpi images from leading digital stock photography companies. There are textures for backgrounds and photos for combining with type or building menu bars, icons or buttons.

Software Contained in this folder are demos and working copies of commercial software. Included are demos from Adobe and MetaTools, and for Macintosh users Equilibrium DeBabelizer. There are also software demos in the WebTools folder.

Contents

For detailed instructions on how to install and use the resources located in the CD-ROM folders, please consult the READ ME, ABOUT or START HERE files in the individual company folders. General installation information is as follows:

WebMagic Files Copy these files to a folder of your choice on your hard drive.

Filters Filters are copied into the Photoshop Plug-ins folder, which is located in the same folder as your Adobe Photoshop application. After copying, restart your computer and then relaunch Photoshop. Select Filter from the menu. These third-party filters will appear at the end of the Adobe standard filters list.

Fonts Fonts are placed into the Fonts Folder, which is located in your System Folder. Open the Font folder on the CD-ROM. Drag the font you would like to try out to your closed System Folder. A message will appear stating that the fonts will be moved to Fonts folder. In the case of Type 1 fonts, you will need to drag both the bitmap and printer files to your closed System Folder. Relaunch Photoshop to use the fonts.

Images and Textures Refer to the READ ME files accompanying each of these collections for instructions about installation. If there are no special instructions, then you can open these files from within Photoshop. Copy those files to the hard drive that you want to access quickly.

A Note about Shareware

Please register and support the shareware concept. Follow the guidelines set forth by the author, including, if required, forwarding a modest shareware payment. Your purchase of this book and accompanying CD-ROM does not release you from this obligation. Refer to the READ ME and other information files which accompany each of the programs for additional information.

Gallery

Backgrounds

Random Tiles, *page 24*

Parquet Tiles, *page 28*

Wave Backgrounds, *page 34*

Tiles on Tiles, *page 38*

Tiling Photos, *page 42*

Type Wallpaper, *page 48*

PostScript Patterns, *page 52*

Diagonal Backgrounds, *page 56*

Titling

OBJECT SHADOWS

Filling Type with an Image, *page 76*

3D Type, *page 80*

Outlined Caps, *page 84*

Initial Caps, *page 88*

Free Transform, *page 92*

Icons

2D Clip Art, *page 98*

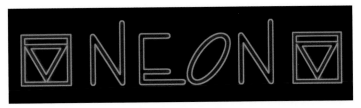

Neon, *page 102*

Rules

Using Custom Brushes, *page 108*

Using Decorative Fonts, *page 112*

Buttons and Bullets

Basic Gradient, *page 116*

Radial Gradients, *page 120*

Bevel, *page 126*

Multicolored Variations, *page 130*

Globe Buttons, *page 136*

Spherized Photos, *page 142*

Gray on Gray, *page 146*

Pill Shaped, *page 152*

Glass, *page 158*

Concentric Circles, *page 162*

Directional Buttons, *page 170*

Objects on Buttons, *page 174*

Menu Bars

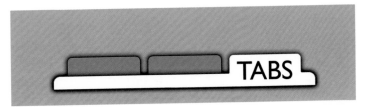

Tabs, *page 180*

Buttons on Image, *page 184*

Gradient Stripes, *page 188*

White on White, *page 192*

Cut Outs, *page 196*

Duotones, *page 200*

Animation

Rotate Animation, *page 206*

Fade On/Off Animation, *page 210*

PEEK A BOO

Write-On Animation, *page 214*

Three Step Marquee Animation, *page 218*

Twirl Animation, *page 224*

GifBuilder

GifBuilder, *page 232*

GIF Construction Set

GIF Construction Set, *page 236*

ADOBE PRESS

Other ADOBE Titles

Adobe Seminars: Web Page Design

All the elements of serving a Web page have been isolated and broken down into accessible components. From buttons to sample CGI scripts, each Web page component is then rebuilt using popular Adobe applications to simulate how Web pages are actually created. The result is a reference book of clear, simple explanations and effective design and production techniques that are reusable page after Web page.

Lisa Lopuck and Sheryl Hampton
1-56830-426-9 ■ $40.00 USA/$57.00 CAN
241 PP
Available Now

Adobe Persuasion: Classroom in a Book
1-56830-316-5 ■ $40.00 US/$56.95 CAN
Available Now

Adobe Premiere for Macintosh: Classroom in a Book, 2E
1-56830-119-7 ■ $49.95 US/$65.95 CAN
Available Now

Adobe Premiere for Windows: Classroom in a Book, 2E
1-56830-172-3 ■ $50.00 US/$68.95 CAN
Available Now

Adobe Pagemill 2.0: Classroom in a Book
1-56830-319-X ■ $40.00 US/$57.00 CAN
Available Now

Adobe After Effects: Classroom in a Book
1-56830-369-6 ■ $45.00 US/$59.00 CAN
Available Now

Interactivity by Design
1-56830-221-5 ■ $40.00 US/$54.95 CAN
Available Now

Internet Publishing with Acrobat
1-56830-300-9 ■ $40.00 US/$54.95 CAN
Available Now

Adobe Illustrator: Classroom in a Book
1-56830-371-8 ■ $45.00 US/$59.00 CAN
Available Now

Adobe Pagemaker: Classroom in a Book
1-56830-370-X ■ $45.00 US/$64.00 CAN
Available Now

Adobe Photoshop: Classroom in a Book
1-56830-371-3 ■ $45.00 US/$59.00 CAN
Available Now

Branding with Type
1-56830-248-7 ■ $18.00 US/$25.00 CAN
Available Now

Adobe Framemaker: Classroom in a Book
1-56830-399-8 ■ $45.00 US/$63.95 CAN
Available Now

Design Essentials, 2E
1-56830-093-X ■ $40.00 US/$54.95 CAN
Available Now

Adobe Designing Business
1-56830-282-7 ■ $60.00 US/$81.95 CAN
Available Now

Stop Stealing Sheep & Find Out How Type Works
0-672-48543-5 ■ $19.95 US/$26.99 CAN
Available Now

MACMILLAN COMPUTER PUBLISHING USA

A VIACOM COMPANY

Technical Support

If you need assistance with the information provided by Macmillan Computer Publishing, please access the information available on our web site at **http://www.mcp.com/feedback.** Our most Frequently Asked Questions are answered there. If you do not find the answers to your questions on our web site, you may contact Macmillan User Services at **(317) 581-3833** or email us at **support@mcp.com**.

REGISTRATION CARD

Photoshop Web Magic, Volume 1

Hayden
Books

Name _____ Title _____

Company_____Type of business _____

Address _____

City/State/ZIP _____

Have you used these types of books before? ☐ yes   ☐ no

If yes, which ones? _____

_____

How many computer books do you purchase each year? ☐ 1–5   ☐ 6 or more

How did you learn about this book? _____

☐ recommended by a friend   ☐ received ad in mail
☐ recommended by store personnel   ☐ read book review
☐ saw in catalog   ☐ saw on bookshelf

Where did you purchase this book? _____

Which applications do you currently use? _____

Which computer magazines do you subscribe to? _____

What trade shows do you attend? _____

Please number the top three factors which most influenced your decision for this book purchase.

☐ cover   ☐ price
☐ approach to content   ☐ author's reputation
☐ logo   ☐ publisher's reputation
☐ layout/design   ☐ other _____

Would you like to be placed on our preferred mailing list? ☐ yes   ☐ no   e-mail address _____

☐ **I would like to see my name in print!** You may use my name and quote me in future Hayden products and promotions. My daytime phone number is: _____

Comments _____
_____
_____

Hayden Books   Attn: Product Marketing ◆ 201 West 103rd Street ◆ Indianapolis, Indiana 46290 USA

Visit our Web Page   **http://WWW.MCP.com**

Fold Here

BUSINESS REPLY MAIL
FIRST-CLASS MAIL PERMIT NO. 9918 INDIANAPOLIS IN
POSTAGE WILL BE PAID BY THE ADDRESSEE

HAYDEN BOOKS
Attn: Product Marketing
201 W 103RD ST
INDIANAPOLIS IN 46290-9058